The Path is Not Always Linear

The Path is Not Always Linear

Practical advice and real-life scenarios to help in your
decision to earn a research doctoral degree

HOLLY J. SCHOENHERR PH.D. AND
RICHARD S. POLLENZ PH.D.

Contents

Foreword

I remember very clearly my decision to apply to a doctoral program. I was twenty-nine years old, working as a clinical speech-language pathologist, and attending art school for multimedia design at night. I was burned out and exhausted, directionless and confused. And then, paging through a random magazine at my allergist's office one day after work, I flipped to an advertisement for a major technology organization that would change my life. The ad gave me a new phrase and, with it, my new field: human factors psychology. Further research confirmed that this subdiscipline of psychology and engineering combined everything that fascinated me. At last, I seemed to have the answer to my perpetual career confusion. I quickly applied to a doctoral program in cognitive psychology at the University of South Florida. I figured the thirty-minute drive from my small condo wouldn't be a big deal.

It was almost a whim, little more than a shot in the dark.

The naivety and hope that propelled me toward the doctorate were enough to get me in the door but certainly weren't enough to help me understand exactly what I was in for. I had no plan, no examples to follow. Armed with only a vague idea that I wanted to design technology, I had virtually no end goals or understanding of how I might bridge the gap between the clinical therapist who dropped an application in the mail and the respected professional *something* I hoped to become. All I knew was that school was my safe place, the place I'd always been successful. Because the world outside academia felt overwhelming, getting a doctorate seemed like a protective haven.

Except, as Drs. Schoenherr and Pollenz so ably articulate, the decision to get a doctorate is not one to take lightly. It's not only possible but probable that you'll quickly find yourself in over your head if you go into a program with inaccurate expectations. The process of getting a doctorate is filled with challenges in the forms of faculty, requirements, school-and-life balance, finances, time, and the sustained dedication necessary. It's not about going to *most* of your classes, studying off and on, living the college life, and hanging out with friends anymore. You don't just cruise to a doctorate; there's no "getting by," even if you've been at the top of your class for as long as you can remember.

The doctorate is about integrating into the intellectual and professional requirements of your chosen field—walking the walk and talking the talk of our deepest thinkers and visionaries. It's about learning to be independent, questioning, innovative, and driven to find answers where there are none. It's about creating new knowledge. More than anything, the doctorate is about being persistent and flexible. This decision is as monumental as our more obvious major life decisions—getting married, having a child, changing careers, moving—and will alter your personal trajectory and perspective forever.

Wouldn't it be helpful to put some thought and care into a decision with such profound implications?

This guide offers the support you need as your knowledgeable mentors Schoenherr and Pollenz walk through the questions you need to ask yourself (and others) to figure out if doctoral education is worth your time and effort. What are the costs? What outcomes are you aiming for? What's a realistic plan?

The plight of students they've advised over the years—like JoAnne, Robert, Karla, and Ren—illustrates common experiences in stark relief. Financial challenges, life on hold, teaching and research competing for your attention, not enough hours in the day, demanding professors: these are the realities of life as a doctoral student. As I read, I found myself chuckling at my astonishing lack of knowledge back in 1998 when I applied ("What? You mean it's difficult to get a faculty position?"). The authors' wise advice and tools will help you understand your interests, mentoring needs, desired benefits, and costs to arrive at a carefully considered decision about whether a doctoral program is right for you.

Now that a doctorate is part of my story, I'm so grateful I made the decision, even if it was rather ill-informed at the time. My program, professors, and peers were instrumental in helping me find the motivated, curious, and independent thinker I am today. If I had to do it over, I'd absolutely do it again, even with all the unforeseen hardships and obstacles. As with any transformational experience, doctoral education certainly requires great sacrifice. Nonetheless, as Robert Frost optimistically suggested, taking the road less traveled can make all the difference for you and the contributions you'll be able to offer the world.

Lucky for you, this book will help you craft your personal map for the journey.

Melanie D. Polkosky, PhD

Author of *Uncovering Truffles: The Scarcity and Value of Women in STEM*

Memphis, Tennessee

Introduction

Statistics from the Council of Graduate Schools show that only about six out of ten students who begin doctoral programs complete the degree within ten years. The reasons that underlie the lack of completion are complex and vary by discipline. However, based on our personal experiences and observations, it is clear that many students who enter graduate school are not fully prepared for what they are getting into, especially at the doctoral level, and have not given sufficient thought to some key questions before entering the program. Our goal is to use our collective fifty-one years of experience in higher education (as students, faculty members, and administrators) to provide information and guidance we believe will be useful in helping you develop a realistic understanding of what graduate school is, what advanced degrees will prepare you for, and how to avoid and overcome some of the common challenges to crossing the finish line.

The purpose of this book is to provide you with information and advice that can help you plan for and work through each milestone of the graduate school journey. Each chapter includes real stories of actual students that provide context to the different issues we cover. (Note that the names of the students in these examples have been changed to protect their identities.) In addition, we have placed action exercises in each chapter that will challenge you to apply the concepts discussed and assess your own motivation, goals, and expectations. It is not essential to read the chapters in order or even to read all the chapters to get the most out of the book. We understand that students who review this book will be coming from a variety of backgrounds and experiences as well as different places in their graduate school journeys. Chapters 1–3 are geared primarily toward students who are not yet enrolled in graduate programs, while chapters 4 and 5 may be most relevant to current graduate students. The chapters do not build on one another, so students may go right to the chapter that is most pertinent and helpful.

In chapter 1, we will share information that may appear very basic but, surprisingly, is not sufficiently understood by many graduate students. Following our presentations on these topics, we often hear students say, "I wish I would have known that earlier." The chapter will explore the types of graduate degrees, career options for those with advanced degrees, responsibilities characteristic of a university professor, and typical trajectories from degree to career. The purpose is to leave you with foundational topics and questions that any student should explore before committing to a graduate program.

In chapter 2, we start to get personal. Life as a graduate student entails personal and professional sacrifices for you and those closest to you. You will be challenged to understand your motivation for pursuing a research-based graduate degree and to think about important issues that will increase the likelihood of successfully completing the program.

Two of the most common questions students ask when considering a graduate program are, "How am I going to pay for this?" and "Is it worth the cost?" Chapter 3 covers a comprehensive array of financial topics that affect graduate students. We explore several factors that affect your return on investment when it comes to earning an advanced degree as well as budgeting for common expenses, earning potential for new assistant professors in various disciplines, debt-management techniques, and the opportunity costs of spending time in graduate school as opposed to pursuing employment.

In chapter 4, you will learn about the importance of doing your homework before enrolling in a particular program and selecting your faculty advisors. We will cover the role of the major advisor and how vital they are to your success. In addition, we will explore common expectations of various disciplines in how students identify the research area that will be the basis of the dissertation.

Finally, chapter 5 will cover some topics around ensuring good habits and discipline to make timely progress and minimize frustrations. We explore themes such as maintaining motivation, managing time effectively, and involving those closest to you to create a solid support structure. We will also challenge you to identify weaknesses that may be holding you back and guide you on how to overcome them.

We recognize that graduate school is far from a one-size-fits-all proposition. This is what we mean when we say that "the path is not always linear!" Therefore, throughout the book, we address differences between master's and doctoral degree programs, between disciplines, and between programs at very-high research universities and other types of institutions. The message you will consistently receive is that your success is largely dependent on your taking the initiative to talk to the right people at your institution or at the institutions you are interested in attending. No book is an adequate substitute for developing relationships with faculty and others who possess the detailed knowledge you will need to successfully complete a research graduate degree. So if you were hoping to read this book and instantly have your life figured out, sorry to disappoint. This book will merely guide you to recommended sources of information and point out action steps that will be important for you to take. This is your journey…make the most of it.

One

What do I want to do with my life?
(a.k.a.: What is graduate school anyway?)

One

WHAT DO I WANT TO DO WITH MY LIFE?
(A.K.A.: WHAT IS GRADUATE SCHOOL ANYWAY?)

JoAnne loved everything about being in college and life at the university. She could see no other position that appealed to her as much as being at a university as a professor. At commencement I saw her walk across the stage and earn her bachelor's degree, and we ran into each other after the event was over. I was expecting her to be full of life and excited for the future, but she was distant and concerned. "I just don't know what the next steps are," she said, "and the dream of earning the doctoral degree just seems so complicated right now." Although JoAnne and I had talked several times about graduate school over the past several years, I was immediately struck by the thought that I had not really helped JoAnne understand how to approach the decision to go to graduate school. I wanted to give her something that would help guide her decision-making process but had never committed to producing such a guide. All I had was my business card. "I am here as a resource and advocate," I said as I gave her a hug and walked away.

Types of graduate degrees

There are many types of graduate degree programs that are designed to provide deeper immersion in a discipline and higher-level certification.

The typical degree trajectory for most disciplines is bachelor's, master's, and then doctorate, with the doctorate being the terminal (highest possible) degree in the discipline. One exception to this is in fine arts, where the master of fine arts (MFA) can be the terminal degree for the discipline. In terms of the progression to the terminal degree, programs in the humanities, education, and social sciences typically require a master's degree to enter a doctoral program. In many STEM (science, technology, engineering, and math) disciplines as well as economics, however, it is possible to enter directly into a doctoral program after earning the bachelor's degree. Because there is no standard formula, it is essential to review the requirements of graduate programs that may be of interest to you. All universities publish detailed information about their graduate programs and the trajectory of each degree. The source for this information is typically found on the graduate schools' websites. Brief descriptions of the different degree programs are provided below.

Master's degrees (e.g., master of arts, MA; master of science, MS). Nearly all disciplines offer master's degrees that build on the discipline beyond the baccalaureate degree. Master's degrees are generally designed to be completed within two to four years and typically require the completion of at least thirty credit hours of coursework. Master's degrees in professional programs such as nursing, public health, business, education, and social work often require up to sixty hours of study and also entail a certification or internship component. In addition, master's programs may require completion of a thesis. Thesis-based master's programs require an original research project and approval of a written thesis or creative project. An important distinction between a thesis-based master's and a nonthesis or undergraduate program is that with a thesis-based program, the degree is conferred only after the successful completion of the research/creative project regardless of the number of credit hours that have been earned.

Professional Science Master's (PSM). In addition to traditional master's degree programs, there is a growing number of PSM programs. PSM programs prepare students for science careers in business, government, or nonprofit organizations. PSM programs combine study in science or mathematics with coursework in management, policy, or law to provide an interdisciplinary experience. Most PSM programs require a final project or an internship in a business or public-sector enterprise. Many PSM programs have placement opportunities directly into the workforce.

Specialist degrees (e.g., education specialist, EdS). Specialist degrees are typically earned in education in addition to a master's degree. A specialist degree may require coursework, training, or internship experience beyond what is required for a master's degree. This type of degree usually prepares students for professional certification or licensing requirements (e.g., EdS for school principal).

Professional doctorates (e.g., doctor of veterinary medicine, DVM; doctor of medicine, MD). The doctor of medicine (MD) degree typifies a professional doctorate program. Professional doctorates are typically completed in a sequential manner over a set number of years (typically three to four). The program combines coursework with internship/practicum training and results in professional certification to practice in the discipline. The ability to practice requires passing the appropriate state and national certification exams. These programs do not require completion of original research or publication; however, many universities offer the opportunity for students to complete both the professional and research doctorate (e.g., MD/PhD) through a single program.

Research doctorates (e.g., doctor of philosophy, PhD; doctor of education, EdD). The terminal degree in most disciplines is the PhD (doctor of philosophy). Some programs in education also offer the EdD (doctor of education). The course requirements for research doctoral programs vary widely across different disciplines, but completion of the coursework is only one component toward earning the degree. PhD programs are classified as research doctoral programs because attainment of the degree *requires* the successful completion of an original research project and the defense of the doctoral dissertation to a faculty committee. Many programs also require peer-reviewed publication of some component of the completed research before the degree will be awarded. The publication requirement is often dependent on the academic discipline and is usually determined by the faculty within the department where the degree will be earned. In contrast to the professional doctorates (such as MD), the time required to earn the PhD degree is open-ended and based on how long it takes to complete and publish the research project, not on when a student has completed a set number of credit hours. For example, if the typical doctoral degree requires a minimum of 90 credits, a full-time student enrolled in a program for five years may earn more than 120 credits (most of which are research credits) by the time the research is defended.

What is the trajectory of the discipline with regard to entry-level career options?

Robert was about a year from completing his PhD in molecular medicine and was angry. "I have been making good progress on the project, and I will meet my 4.5-year timeline to graduate," he said. "But my goal to be a professor at a medical school looks very far in the future." Robert had arrived at the university after receiving his BS from a small college that did not have a strong research focus or medical school. Now as he was getting close to earning his PhD, it had become clear that he would need to complete another three to four years of postdoctoral training in a new research area before he could even apply for a tenure-track position at a high-level research university. I asked him whether he had researched the trajectory to a faculty position in a medical school before he had arrived. He confessed that he had thought earning the PhD was the last step toward such a position and that many of the faculty at his undergraduate institution had been employed right after earning their PhDs. He said that if he had known then what he knew now, he might have made different choices since he was married and had a two-year-old child.

Robert's tale is an important case study because it highlights the importance of not only understanding how attaining the graduate degree provides opportunities toward different careers but also understanding how the degree credentials you for entry-level positions in academia. Robert did not have all the information he needed and mistakenly thought he could obtain a faculty position right away after graduating. In reality, the position he was talking about, a faculty-level research position in a medical school, remains one of the most competitive positions for individuals earning PhDs in biomedical fields. To be competitive for these positions, it is typical to spend three to five years training as a postdoctoral scholar *after* earning the PhD.

Perhaps you have similar goals. What do you know about the process of obtaining a faculty position and its duties? Will earning the PhD actually be a direct entry point for you, or will additional training and/or licensure be required for several years *after* earning the degree? Alternatively, perhaps you are already enrolled in your program and have observed the duties of your major professor and are now questioning whether an academic career is something that excites you as much as you thought it would. Helping students understand the pathways to various careers is an issue that is now receiving increased attention at the national level. In the near future, universities may be required to provide disciplinary career information upon entry to the program, but we are not there yet. The good news is that all disciplines have multiple career options that can be explored, and it is never too late to research this information.

What, then, is the best advice on how to determine the career trajectories and options that would be available for individuals who hold degrees in particular disciplines? One strategy is to think about people you know who are in careers that appeal to you. Reach out to those people. Ask them how they got into their careers and what their pathways were. You may be surprised to learn that their career pathways were not as linear as you thought and that those you speak with may have held many different jobs along the way. You will also find that most people are willing to provide information about their career experiences and how they made key decisions about the paths to take. We have on occasion provided short interviews on our career paths to both undergraduate and graduate students who were compiling such information into a database. No matter where you are in your life, this is something you can do. Make it a habit to engage in conversation about careers. The pathway to careers should also be a question that is high on your list when you interview for graduate school or visit a university.

If you are already enrolled in a graduate degree program, you have access to resources within the graduate school and the career center. Most doctoral-granting universities offer these services and provide workshops and training to help students understand career pathways. This information is typically advertised on the websites for those offices. In addition, you should speak directly with the administrative staff of the graduate school and your academic college about career pathways. If you are not ready to engage at that level, another option is to review the curricula vitae (CVs) of faculty in disciplines of interest to you. This information is readily available at most universities and provides a wealth of information about the time faculty members spent in graduate school and the paths they took to their current positions.

Unfortunately, it is impossible to outline a complete list of different career paths in this book, and historically there has been a lack of comprehensive research on the multitude of careers students enter after earning a graduate degree. However, we can provide some information that will assist you in understanding general pathways and timelines to careers in academia. Figure 1 shows the timelines for attaining the doctoral degree across broad disciplinary areas and whether additional postdoctoral training, publication, and funding are typically required to obtain an academic position. We hope this information will provide a starting point for you to make informed decisions about your professional training, research, and teaching while you are engaged in your doctoral program. We have observed that the most successful graduate students understand these trajectories when they begin their programs (unlike Robert), have career plans, and use all the resources available at the university to receive the widest array of credentialing. As stated earlier, the step-by-step path to most jobs is not something that is readily published, and there are always exceptions to how someone attained a position. But the more you can become informed by talking to faculty, staff, administrators, and fellow students, the more you will be empowered to take control of your career and become an informed consumer.

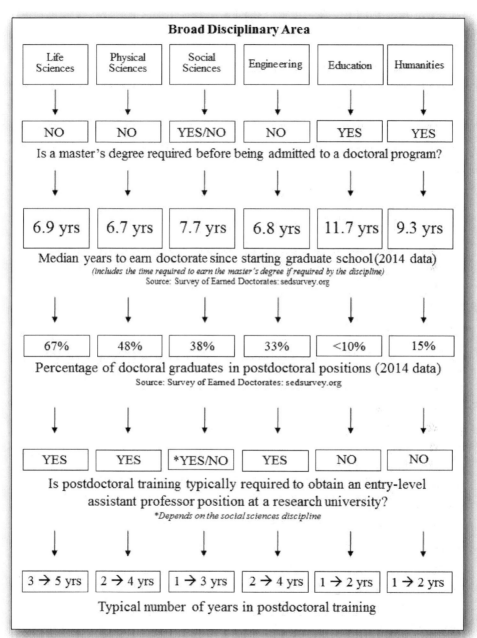

Figure 1. Trajectory to Doctoral Degree Completion and Entry-Level Academic Positions.

What do you know about tenure, faculty duties, and the professoriate?

Soon after Sandra's admission to the doctoral program, she met with the department chair to learn more about the faculty members in the department to inform her decision about which ones she should ask to serve on her advisory committee and, more importantly, which one to request as her major advisor. Sandra explained to the department chair that she was not yet sure of the research question she wanted to explore for her dissertation but was interested in the areas of educational leadership and faculty development. The department chair commented that Dr. Graves would have been a suitable advisor because his research interests were very much aligned with Sandra's, and he had a good reputation for his mentorship of students. However, Dr. Graves was not taking on any more students because he had recently been denied tenure and, therefore, would be leaving the department at the end of the academic year. Sandra did ultimately identify a very good advisor, but when I spoke with her a few years later, she said she felt very lucky to have a chair who was willing to help her learn about department structure and that she had never realized how much she did not know about the day-to-day life of a tenure-track faculty member.

Classifications of faculty and tenure. One of the aspects of a faculty career that makes it unique from most other industries is the tenure process. Just as doctoral students must meet various milestones to graduate, such as the production of a quality dissertation, so must faculty meet a certain level of quality in areas of teaching, research, and service to be awarded tenure. In fact, a faculty lifestyle is not all that dissimilar to that of a graduate student. There are constant demands to produce high-quality scholarly publications and/or research while balancing a teaching load. Sandra's story is not uncommon but has an upside because she was able to engage a tenured faculty member as her dissertation advisor. However, the story highlights the importance of understanding faculty rank as you consider whether you want to obtain such a position in the future and the importance of selecting faculty who will advise you during your graduate career. The selection of a dissertation advisor is discussed in detail in chapter 4.

There are three levels of the tenure-earning professorship: assistant professor, associate professor, and full professor. The path to each of these positions and the duties will vary depending on the type of institution, but we will cover some general expectations here as they pertain to a large research university. The entry level for the professoriate is at the rank of assistant professor. This position is intended to last five to seven years. During this time, the faculty member must develop an independent research program and produce scholarly work, such as peer-reviewed journal articles, to meet specific disciplinary benchmarks set by the university. The faculty member is also expected to maintain high-quality teaching and engage in service to the university. The university can determine not to renew the contract of the assistant professor after each academic year. After five to six years, the assistant professor is expected to compile a portfolio of information about their research, teaching, and service to the university. The portfolio also contains letters from faculty at other universities who indicate whether the candidate would earn tenure at their institution. The portfolio is evaluated by the departmental faculty; college tenure committee; and senior leadership of the university and possibly the board of trustees, who ultimately approve or deny the portfolio. If viewed favorably, the assistant professor is granted tenure and promoted to the rank of associate professor. An award of tenure means the faculty member cannot be dismissed without just cause or extreme financial exigency of the institution, both of which are usually very difficult for a college or university to demonstrate. However, the department or college may adjust the duties of the associate professor based on the level of performance in any given area. Promotion to the rank of full professor is a similar process and at a research university requires that the individual demonstrate significant national and international recognition for the scholarship in their discipline.

A key point to understand is that it is in a university's interest for tenure-track faculty to succeed. Therefore, universities typically provide resources and support to aid assistant professors with teaching and research. Some departments have a very proactive approach to the mentorship and training of junior faculty, but many do not. Ultimately, identifying career mentors and engaging in professional development end up being the responsibilities of the faculty member. Many of the junior faculty we know who did not earn tenure failed to do so in part because they did not fully understand what the job entailed, tried do it all themselves, and did not take advantage of all the resources that were available to help them succeed. This is why it is so critical to understand how a department functions and the quality of the department chair, tenured faculty, and graduate program director. Strong departments put faculty in these mentorship roles who are proactive and supportive of graduate students in their program and willing to assist all members of the department in understanding what it means to succeed in an academic setting.

As you engage with the more successful faculty at your university, you will instantly observe a passion for the work they are doing, engagement with the university, a genuine interest to work with students, and a clear and prolific research agenda (as applicable to the type of institution). Although the success or happiness of the faculty you meet is important to understand, the real question is, are *you* passionate about pursuing this type of position? It is easy to make assumptions about what life would be like as a professor and underestimate the demands of a faculty career until you are in the throes of the first year or two of a tenure-track position. The more you know about the profession and the career trajectories before you even enter the graduate program, the better prepared you will be to ask important questions and make relevant observations as you work toward your degree.

Typical faculty duties. At nearly all higher-education institutions, the duties of faculty fall into three main categories that include teaching, research, and service. The percentage of effort devoted to each of these areas depends on the type of institution. For example, a faculty at a large research university may spend 55 percent on research, 40 percent on teaching, and 5 percent on service, while at a primarily undergraduate university, the percentages may be 80 percent teaching, 10 percent research, and 10 percent service and advising. In the ideal scenario, these three assignments work to complement one another and provide benefits to students, institutions, and faculty. A professor heavily engaged in research may reflect their passion for research in their teaching and, as a consequence, inspire students about the discipline and provide deeper immersion into it. Unfortunately, many students see the faculty only in their teaching roles and do not realize they are being instructed by world-class researchers who are also involved in many other types of activities at the university. The repertoire of activities includes teaching classes, conducting research, attending and presenting at professional conferences, mentoring graduate and undergraduate students, serving on department or university committees, and engaging in administrative duties. The flexibility to develop and manage an independent research program and engage in the variety of other duties is what makes a faculty position at a research university an appealing and challenging position.

The expectations for research productivity vary depending on the discipline and type of institution. The term "research" generally refers to all forms of discovery and scholarly/creative activities specific to the discipline. With rare exception, tenure-track faculty at research universities are expected to maintain an active progression of scholarship and creative activities as defined by the discipline and attain national and international recognition for their work. The ability to obtain extramural funding to support the research program is also a significant expectation for tenure-track faculty at a research university. Faculty in the STEM fields are required to obtain significant external funding for their research and must demonstrate the ability to maintain funding for their programs to be promoted. Because the level of federal funding available to support research outside of STEM disciplines is more limited, the requirements to obtain funding in non-STEM disciplines is often dependent on the specific discipline and stature of the university and department. You are encouraged to fully explore this aspect of being a tenure-track faculty member through discussions with professors and research on the web. Most research universities have a research office with a number of resources about the type and level of funding in each department and college. If you are pursuing a graduate degree in a STEM discipline, it is imperative that you know the funding history of faculty in your department, one of whom may serve as your dissertation advisor and realize that if you aspire to the same type of position, you will face similar funding expectations.

The teaching load that is assigned to a tenure-track faculty member will depend on the department and type of institution. However, regardless of the institution, the development and delivery of both graduate and undergraduate courses will certainly be a component of any tenure-track position and a requirement for promotion. The full range of responsibilities that encompass teaching is also something that is important to understand and is often not apparent while simply taking a course. Most tenure-track faculty are responsible for every aspect of their courses. This includes, but is not limited to, choosing the course-delivery platform (online or in person), selecting reading materials, developing all course content, developing the course website, preparing and managing all assessments, attending office hours and answering student e-mails, managing teaching assistants, and providing information about student learning outcomes for university accreditation. Faculty may also be assigned to teach courses with large enrollments (one hundred or more students). Although a large enrollment course may have only three lecture hours during the week, management of the course and interactions with students may involve twenty to thirty hours of the professor's time per week. At a large research university, faculty are expected to do all this while maintaining a full-time research program as discussed above. Is this what you have imagined?

"I have no idea how you manage to get the work done." It was Dr. Smitten, a new faculty member we had hired about a year prior. "I just feel that I can never catch up!" I had been trying to have him meet me for lunch, but he always found an excuse to miss it. As someone who had successfully made it through the tenure process and navigated the balance between research and teaching, I wanted to help him, but he needed to commit to getting together. He also needed to identify some good doctoral students so he could assure the research would move forward. He ultimately did connect with me and other faculty and turned out to be very willing to listen to our stories of success and failure and to learn how to create the time and balance he needed to be successful.

While many research professors have highly developed skills in both teaching and research, the effort devoted to teaching is often one of the most difficult areas to balance for a new assistant professor since the chair and dean typically say that a successful tenure and promotion decision is primarily based on scholarship and funding. As you consider a tenure-track position, think about your academic experiences and the courses you have taken as an undergraduate or graduate student. You likely have experienced very passionate and dedicated professors as well as others who did not seem to be fully engaged. Have you spoken with your favorite professors, and do you know whether they are research faculty or purely instructional faculty? If becoming a research professor is your dream, what is your passion for teaching, and have you considered how you will balance this with your research? If you have little or no experience in the craft of curriculum development and teaching, how do you know it is something you want to make a career out of? Will you have the opportunity to engage in professional development and obtain teaching opportunities while in your graduate program? A thorough exploration of all these questions can help you become informed as you make decisions about your career goals.

The last duty of a tenure-track position that is important to understand is loosely defined as service. Service is perhaps the most underemphasized and misunderstood part of faculty responsibilities. It is important to understand that a typical university is structured into academic colleges that might be termed College of Arts and Sciences, College of Natural Science, College of Education, College of Fine Arts, and so on. Within each college, there are departments of faculty that usually are focused in a specific discipline, such as philosophy, psychology, biology, or mechanical engineering. Thus, service can include effort that supports the disciplinary profession, department, academic college, or university. Service to the disciplinary profession may take many forms, including participating in professional academic organizations, serving on a grant review panel, reviewing articles or books for publication, or serving as a journal editor. Each department functions through a department chair who relies on committees of departmental faculty to provide advice, schedule the seminar series, or manage searches for new faculty and/or staff. Service to academic colleges may include participation on various committees that advise the dean or make decisions about graduate and undergraduate curriculum. Finally, service to the university includes involvement in the faculty senate, assessment council, library, accreditation, or another assignment that serves the *whole* university.

While some institutions put a special emphasis on service, this component of a typical faculty member's duties is usually assigned less than 10 percent of their effort. However, engaging in committee and governance work can be immensely important and is critical in developing key networking relationships with deans and other important administrators. In addition, serving on college and university committees provides an opportunity to actually learn how the university functions, understand shared governance, and participate in decisions that affect the entire university. As a graduate student, you also have the opportunity to serve on committees and learn about all aspects of the university. This provides an exceptional networking opportunity and will challenge you regarding commitment and time management. You may want to participate in many interesting initiatives, but you will not be able to take on everything and should not do so until you have established yourself in your program. It may seem ironic, but the way in which you manage your graduate research and academics with committee involvement and other activities is exactly the same challenge faced by a beginning faculty member!

The legacy issue and alternatives to academic faculty careers

Serya had been working in an administrative position at a research university for five years when she started the PhD program in higher-education administration. Although she thoroughly enjoyed academic administration, throughout the program she waivered back and forth about whether she should be more open to the possibility of pursuing a tenure-track faculty position once she had the degree. Her perception was that there seemed to be limited potential for career growth in academic administration without achieving tenure as a faculty member. To have a shot at a tenure-track position, she knew she would need to publish and present research at conferences and have some teaching experience. After spending a semester as an adjunct professor, she realized that teaching was not her passion, and it would be better to refocus her energies into applying her degree directly to administrative opportunities.

While many students do pursue careers in the professoriate after completion of their degrees, there are many other options for individuals with doctoral degrees beyond the tenure-track faculty position. Employers include state and federal government agencies, primary and secondary education, the private sector, nonprofits, and of course colleges and universities. Serya found she was qualified for numerous nonfaculty positions within university administration that were a great match to her skills, and she ultimately took a position as human resources director at a medium-size comprehensive public university. According to the Council of Graduate Schools, about half of new PhDs enter careers outside of academe. The percentages vary by discipline, but the data show that individuals with doctoral degrees in science, engineering, and health-related disciplines are more likely to work in business and industry, and those with degrees in the humanities are most likely to take traditional faculty positions at colleges and universities. Many nonacademic organizations seek employees with doctoral degrees for a variety of reasons. Successful completion of the degree indicates you have developed certain skills and experiences, including critical thinking; writing; information synthesis; and the ability to identify, frame, and systematically analyze problems. Employers also see PhDs as valuable because of their tolerance for ambiguity and ability to manage stress. If you are interested in nonacademic positions, your focus should be on building experiences in leadership, project and people management, effective oral and written communication, and grant writing.

Although faculty in your discipline can be an excellent resource on what it means to be a professor, you should not assume they will be able to fully educate you on careers outside of the academy. This is not because they do not want to be good mentors. Rather, you should recognize that the faculty in your department may have moved directly into a tenure-track position following graduate school and remained at the institution where they earned tenure. Also, consider that within their professional circles, they may network with other faculty members who share similar job experiences. A great place to research the career paths of faculty is by reviewing their curricula vitae (CVs). Through this process you may identify individuals who have worked outside the academy or have networking contacts who would be of great benefit as you think about careers.

Another important concept to understand is that the culture of the academic environment may put academic careers on a pedestal. This attitude may cause students who wish to pursue nonacademic employment opportunities to feel like second-class citizens or that they are "settling" for a lower-tier employment opportunity. Some professors view their mentoring role with expectations that their students will become like them (legacy graduates), and students can feel the pressures that come with those expectations. This narrow view of success varies by discipline. The choice of the dissertation advisor can be especially important if you know that you plan to pursue a nonacademic career. In the end, remember that graduate school is temporary, and you likely will pursue your chosen career for many years afterward. In many cases, the path is not linear, and it has been proven time and time again that if you have earned the terminal degree and have both skills and passion, you can get to your promised land from many directions. It is much more important that you have peace about your career choice rather than trying to live up to anyone else's expectations.

Due to the ever-changing job market and array of opportunities across all disciplines, it is not possible to provide a comprehensive listing of jobs that would cover every discipline. Also, new types of jobs are being created every day. Due to the impact of the global economy and advancements in technology, there are many jobs that will be available when you complete your degree that do not even exist today. Although the investment in a graduate degree will almost always allow credentialing for a position that will offset the investment, such a return on investment is predicated on actually getting the position. As we have suggested throughout this chapter, it is important that you do your homework on career options and what those jobs typically pay before committing yourself to the graduate program. When you are ready to explore possible careers relevant to your discipline, you may want to check out the following sources for more information.

The Chronicle of Higher Education website (www.chronicle.com) is an excellent source for information on careers. The Chronicle publishes many articles related to both academic and nonacademic jobs for individuals with terminal degrees. In addition, they post a variety of positions that will be of interest to individuals with advanced degrees, and you may search for career options both within academia and "organizations other than colleges." Another helpful resource is the Council of Graduate Schools (www.cgsnet. org). The Council has recently given increased attention to career options for individuals with advanced degrees. Their 2012 study entitled "Pathways Through Graduate School and Into Careers" explored the transition from degree completion to a variety of career possibilities. In addition, a simple Internet search will lead you to blogs and websites created by individuals who have been where you are and are happy to share lessons learned via the web.

The US Department of Labor website is also an excellent resource for publications and data on employment trajectories, predicted job growth, and compensation. If you are in the process of selecting a graduate program, spending some time on this site will be a great benefit in your decision-making process. Most institutions also have a career center with staff who specialize in helping students understand career options and provide professional development training that will assist in securing a position.

Chapter 1 action items

In many of the professional development workshops we do for students, we help them create an action plan that guides the decision-making process and includes the setting of realistic goals that will be completed over a specific timeline. The exercise below is designed to assist you in collecting information that will help you make decisions from an informed perspective versus working from perceptions.

DEVELOPING AN ACTION PLAN.

- *Determine all the requirements for the degree you are going to pursue by visiting with the department graduate director or the university's graduate school:*

- Does the degree program require the completion of a defined research project?
- What is the typical timeline for completion?
- Do you need to complete a master's degree before you enter the doctoral program?
- Does completion of the degree allow direct entry into the career option you wish to pursue?

- *Engage in discussions with faculty and professionals about their career trajectories.* We once worked with two students who kept journals of short interviews they did with faculty about their career trajectories and decisions.
- *If you desire to pursue an academic position, engage in discussions with faculty about the duties and values of their positions.* We have seen students pursue alternate pathways based on these types of conversations and the realization that they did not want to do that type of job.
- *Visit a university career center and review the US Department of Labor website to research projected career opportunities for your degree.* You may find other types of jobs you did not even know existed.
  - Are you willing to consider a range of career options? If so, what are they?
  - Do they all require the same level of degree?
- *If you are currently enrolled in an undergraduate or graduate program, pursue opportunities to serve on a university committee.* One of the best ways to gain experience with how a university works is to serve on a university committee. The experience can be transformative and also reveal career opportunities that you had not previously considered.

Two

How do I know that a research doctoral degree is right for me?

Two

HOW DO I KNOW THAT A RESEARCH DOCTORAL DEGREE IS RIGHT FOR ME?

Introduction

Early in the second year of his PhD graduate program in cell biology, Joseph sat in my office with his head in his hands. "Graduate school was a big mistake," he said. "I really thought that I knew about the time commitment based on the course schedule that I reviewed before I accepted the admission offer. I did not realize that I was expected to make research progress so soon and spend so much time in the lab. My wife is really upset with me about all the time I am spending here at school." Although Joseph was in good academic standing, I had already received a complaint from his faculty mentor about his lack of research progress and insufficient time commitment. The situation called for immediate intervention before it further deteriorated the student-faculty relationship and soured Joseph's passion for the discipline. In addition, would remaining in the program result in continued tensions between Joseph and his wife?

Unfortunately this story is not uncommon. National statistics show that only about 60 percent of doctoral students complete their degrees within ten years of entering their programs (Council of Graduate Schools Doctoral Completion Project). Although the reasons students do not complete are varied and complex, the statistic is still staggering when one considers the investment of funding in doctoral education by the university and the significant time commitment of the students and mentors. A major question that graduate program directors and graduate deans are asking is, "What can be done to better prepare students prior to their arrival in the program?" We have encountered a growing number of doctoral students who have entered graduate school without really knowing anything about the university, the program, the faculty, or what they actually need to accomplish in the program. In Joseph's case, he may have been able to ask better questions and make a more informed decision if he had engaged in a self-assessment and researched what graduate school would be like before making his decision to attend. He would also have benefited from becoming familiar with the faculty in his program and then reaching out to one or two of them rather than simply reviewing the program's web page.

We are strong proponents of self-assessment exercises because we believe they are critical to making good decisions that affect finances, career, and family. Self-assessment exercises may be in the form of a SWOT analysis (strengths, weaknesses, opportunities, and threats) or a risk assessment, but the purpose of any self-assessment exercise is to help an individual or group articulate goals and information that will facilitate identification of priorities and informed decision making. When Joseph was asked whether he and his wife had engaged in a self-assessment, he confessed there had been little analysis beyond looking for a program he could get into after he was denied medical-school admission. Since we often give workshops on attending graduate school to prospective students, there was the ability to access a PowerPoint that contained a graduate school self-assessment. The questions were created to address issues that repeatedly came up in our discussions with undergraduate and graduate students. Joseph was provided the questions and asked to go through them with his wife. He was encouraged to provide honest and thoughtful answers and advised that to do the exercise meaningfully would require a few hours of time. He was also cautioned that he might not like some questions because they would expose deficiencies in his understanding of graduate school and where his career was headed. The guiding questions Joseph utilized are used to frame each of the following sections and are also provided in the self-assessment exercise at the end of this chapter. In each section we provide context for the respective question to explain why it is important in your decision-making process.

What is my motivation to attend graduate school?

Jade's motivation to pursue a doctorate was purely opportunistic. Because of the tuition benefit offered by her employer, she could complete the degree with minimal out-of-pocket cost. When her husband suggested (at the commencement ceremony where she received her MBA) that she pursue a doctorate, Jade thought he was crazy. He had taken up the load of raising their young son while Jade pursued the MBA, and now, after welcoming a second son into the world just five days earlier, he was suggesting that they go through it all over again. How could Jade pass up the opportunity to put herself in a more marketable professional position, especially considering the strong support structure she obviously had in her personal life... but were those good enough reasons to do it?

Graduate school is difficult and filled with complexities; you should not enroll lightly. If you were to survey the students in any graduate program about the factors that motivated them to enroll, you will likely encounter a wide variety of responses. Thinking back to our graduate school days, it was interesting to talk to fellow classmates and listen to the stories of their journeys to graduate school. There were the younger students who had very little work experience in the field and pretty much dove right into the doctoral program after receiving a master's degree, while at the other end of the spectrum were the older students who had put in many years behind a desk in the academic, corporate, or nonprofit world. We found these older students to be particularly inspiring because their motivations to complete the program were not centered around jump-starting their careers but rather pursuing their passions and desires for greater intellectual challenge.

Are you motivated to get a graduate degree because of your passion for solving a particular research question? Are you trying to obtain additional credentialing that will help you advance in an already-established career? Are you attending because this is something others want you to do? Do you feel that this is your road to riches? Or is graduate school a fallback option because you did not get the job you wanted or get into a professional school? There are no right or wrong answers, but understanding your true motivations for pursuing the degree will help you succeed and ultimately graduate. Students who have an internal passion for the discipline and a strong desire to build a career based on the field of study are more likely to complete the degree than those who attend graduate school for extrinsic reasons. Also, it is essential that you engage other stakeholders (significant other, family members, etc.) in the discussion so they can understand your motivation and have an opportunity to support your decision. This is *not* a decision to make in a vacuum.

Am I choosing a research doctoral program as my first option?

At first glance this may appear to be a rather benign question, but asking it and answering honestly are critical. In Joseph's case, he had wanted to get into an MD program and later told me that graduate school was his fallback option. After working on the self-assessment questions with his wife, he discovered she had been counting on him to earn the medical degree. Some of her frustrations with him were related to her perception that he had settled for graduate school and the PhD. It was clear she did not understand what he could actually do with this doctoral degree and that he could still dramatically influence the health field as a researcher in a medical school.

If you are in the same situation as Joseph because you did not get into a professional doctoral program like medical school, your passion toward the degree may be less than what it would be if you were pursuing your degree of first choice. Although this should in no way discourage you from pursuing a research doctorate, it is important to determine whether you understand what is ahead and whether you have the needed motivation and commitment to see it through.

A good exercise that puts this question in context is to think about basic tasks that you do now on a regular basis. There are some tasks you thoroughly enjoy and some you do not, but in most cases, you do the undesirable tasks only because there are more undesirable consequences if you do not. For example, if you do not find enjoyment and satisfaction in cleaning your bathroom, you may avoid the task or do just enough to avoid noticeable consequences. In other words, it is likely you will not put your best effort into cleaning the bathroom and will not clean it as often as you should if doing it does not give you personal satisfaction. Conversely, if you engage in an activity you enjoy, then you will likely not put it off but rather will commit your full effort to it even if it is difficult to do.

The point of this example is that if you are not committed to earning your PhD and feel you have settled for it, then you are likely to lack the motivation to do your very best work or prioritize the time for your studies ahead of other demands. This is not to say that students who lack strong internal motivation should not pursue a degree. You should recognize, however, that you will encounter greater challenges than a fellow classmate who is fired up about the research they are pursuing in the discipline. Success in graduate school does not come easy and requires a great deal more self-motivation than the undergraduate degree. Consider this as you evaluate your answer: a component of all doctoral research is publication and presentation. How will you inspire others to invest in and advocate for you if you are not inspired and passionate about your research project and general discipline?

What do I want to accomplish in my career?

Sean originally entered the accounting program because he was told that accounting is the language of business, and since he wanted to eventually start his own business, he figured speaking the business language would be useful. As he made his way through the first few terms and courses, he found himself convinced that a PhD would open all the doors to a prestigious career in a big-name accounting firm. On top of that, he truly enjoyed the intellectual challenge and the opportunity to engage in research.

As Sean drew closer to completing his coursework, he came to a crossroads. He had the opportunity to start a small business, and the adrenaline created a feeling of excitement he had never experienced as a doctoral student, prompting him to leave the PhD program. His decision to leave had nothing to do with a dislike for the work as a doctoral student or the idea of a career teaching college students. Instead, it was about being brutally honest with himself and realizing he had goals, desires, and passions he wanted to pursue more than he wanted the degree.

If you are contemplating enrolling or have already enrolled in a doctoral program, it is likely because you believe the degree will enhance your career opportunities. What are your career goals? Not every student has aspirations for a faculty position, but that is arguably the most common goal for doctoral students in many disciplines. Keep in mind that the purpose of this book is to provide you with resources and self-reflection tools that will help you make informed decisions before, during, and after you engage in a graduate program. One desired outcome is to help you through the process of thinking *beyond your degree* so you can take advantage of opportunities that will enhance your curriculum vitae and increase your chances of pursuing your target vocation.

When Karla was asked in her interview for admission to graduate school why she wanted to get a PhD, she explained that the PhD was required for her to attain a faculty position at a university. She did not speak to the specific research she wanted to pursue, per se, but rather approached attaining the PhD degree as a means to academic employment opportunities that would otherwise be closed to her. Karla's vision statement was related to teaching science at a small liberal arts university and contained no mention of molecular biology research.

Fifteen years later, Karla had established herself as a respected research professor. Despite her original vision to teach at a liberal arts college,

Karla opened herself up to research opportunities in graduate school and discovered she was actually quite skilled as a research scientist. And she discovered that the reason she was good at it was because she was passionate about it. Following her passion for research predominately defined Karla's faculty career. Later on, Karla again kept herself open to new challenges and accepted an academic administration position that now provides her with opportunities to engage in program development and influence teaching as stated in her original vision statement.

The poet and social activist Langston Hughes said, "I have discovered in life that there are ways of getting almost anywhere you want to go, if you really want to go." The path is not always linear! You are more likely to succeed in graduate school and in securing the type of job that most appeals to you if you take some time to outline what it is that will make for a satisfying career. Any self-help book on goal setting will emphasize the importance of having a clear vision of the desired outcome prior to determining the pathway to achieve your goals.

Your vision is a picture of your ideal future. To help provide clarity to your career vision, we suggest you write a brief vision statement. The guidelines to help you through this exercise are provided in the "Chapter 2 action items" section at the end of this chapter. This is a powerful exercise as articulating your thoughts creatively will help you to think through what is most meaningful to you. A written vision statement, if kept somewhere visible, can be a helpful reminder and reinforcement for why you are going through graduate school. This should be a living document, and a career vision statement may undergo several drafts before you feel satisfied with the final product. The development of your vision statement should not be rushed. Take your time with it. You do not have to complete it in one sitting, but you should not drag it out so long that you neglect it altogether. Your initial draft should be fairly open to ideas, both rational and irrational. This is a right-brain exercise, so don't let pragmatism and logic get in the way.

Once you have documented your thoughts, refine your vision statement so the final product is no more than two to four sentences. You should also keep your vision statement in a place where you will see it often and be able to reflect on whether your goals and actions are supporting your vision. Since this is a living document, you should also come back to it over time and revise it if your priorities or values change, but don't give in to the pressure to alter your vision statement in light of current negative circumstances. Remember that your vision statement is based on your definition of success, not on circumstances or what others believe is best for you.

What research areas truly inspire me?

Some students are clear about the specialization they wish to pursue in their discipline and decide on a specific research focus before entering a doctoral program. Others enter the program with a general idea of their interests and discover or develop a research project after being exposed to core courses and engaging in discussions with faculty, students, and postdoctoral scholars. Regardless of which category you fall into, you must have a burning passion for the research that defines your degree, so it is essential to become familiar with the entire list of faculty associated with your prospective graduate program (and those programs that cross your discipline) to gain an understanding of their research interests, extramural funding history (if applicable), and scholarship (publication and presentation). To restate a common theme we hope you are learning throughout this book, *the better informed you are, the better you will be at making key decisions.*

The type of research that is available to you as a doctoral student is limitless and constrained only by your own creativity and desire. The disciplines differ in how research projects are developed (see chapter 4 for a detailed description of the process for different disciplines), but the constant across all disciplines is the requirement that you must be engaged in research you truly *want* to do. You can find details about all types of research being carried out at a university by mining the departmental websites and reviewing the faculty profiles or by using any search engine or your university library to simply explore specific topic areas more globally.

Passion and drive are critical in successfully completing a research doctoral program because you will need a high level of both to get you through the frustration and drudgery you will surely encounter at various points along the way. In addition, unlike an undergraduate degree that is earned by obtaining a specific GPA within a specified set of credit hours, all research doctoral programs require completion of an original research project. The completion of the dissertation project and its successful defense are what determine whether the degree is granted, not how many credit hours have been earned. It is also important to understand and accept that the pathway to completion is not linear. The desire to solve the research question is critical at all times and is especially important when the project is stalled and you feel the urge to give up. Ask yourself, "Will this research project inspire me to get up each day to face the next set of challenges?" A burning passion of inquiry and discovery will get you through and also allow you to inspire others about what you do!

Do I have geographical, work, or personal considerations that need to be addressed?

The offer from the prestigious school in the Midwest was too good to turn down. Although Younghoon's wife had agreed with the decision to accept the offer, he knew she did not like cold weather and that she would need to find a new job. During his first year, Younghoon struggled academically because he was concerned about his wife's ability to adapt to the new city and find a job. In addition, he now had a forty-five-minute commute that cut into the amount of time he could spend with her. The departmental graduate director was concerned about Younghoon's lack of academic progress and cautioned that he was close to being dismissed from the program. He was also in danger of being unable to identify a major professor because his work ethic was being questioned. Fortunately, Younghoon's wife was able to get a job at the university, and they began to commute together. In addition, they worked together to establish a schedule of household chores and identified times they could spend together but that still enabled Younghoon to focus on academics and research.

Younghoon's story illustrates how the decision to commit to a research doctoral program can affect many aspects of your life. Many students get caught up in being admitted to their choice school without considering important personal factors. The location of the university, its proximity to family, the availability of jobs, the location of housing, or the climate may be very important factors to consider even if admission to the graduate program appears to be a dream opportunity. Keeping these topics in the conversation is especially important if you have a partner or family who will be leaving a current job or school to move with you. If your priorities are inconsistent with those of your partner, then serious discord may ensue. If you are single, exploring these issues is equally important, and you should weigh the benefits and costs related to moving to the new setting and decide whether the benefits outweigh the costs. Only you can make that determination. In the story above, there was still a significant period of adjustment and compromise that Younghoon and his wife had to work through, even though it had been a joint decision for him to take the position. Fortunately, as the couple worked together through the issues, they were able to create a very positive situation because they worked as a team and continued to communicate with each other.

What are my financial assumptions and projections?

The cost of a graduate degree is clearly one of the most critical issues that must be considered and resolved when making your decision to attend graduate school. While estimating the cost for the degree, you must consider that the time to complete a research doctoral program is not defined and is based on completion of an original research project versus a specified number of courses. As shown in chapter 1, the typical time to complete a doctoral degree is six to ten years.

The good news is that for most disciplines, the return on investment for a doctoral degree is high when you consider the average compensation paid to those with doctoral degrees in academia and the private sector. In addition, the average unemployment rate for individuals with doctoral degrees is much lower than for those with bachelor's or master's degrees (consult the most recent statistics from the Department of Labor). The bottom line is that you must do your homework on the financial considerations and engage in conversations with your partner and those in the graduate programs you are considering. In chapter 3 we provide guiding questions to assist you in understanding financial resources available to help fund your graduate studies.

How much time am I willing to invest?

Humberto had arrived at the university early on a Sunday morning to complete the analysis of his protein samples. Since his major professor shared the analysis equipment with another faculty member and it was located in their lab, Humberto had asked one of the graduate students to leave the key to the lab on his desk. However, when he got to his desk, there was no key. This had happened before, and unlike other students who might have simply gone home and not completed the analysis, he was able to get into the lab by using a thin piece of film to unlock the door.

Let's face this one straight on: committing to a research doctorate typically means you are willing to work way beyond full-time (forty hours a week) to complete the research project. As discussed in chapter 1, earning a research-based degree (PhD or thesis-master's) is dependent on completing an original research project rather than earning a set number of credit hours. There are also programs that require publication of the research before the degree will be conferred. The total time commitment to completing the degree is significant. The median time to earn the degree from the beginning of the graduate program ranges from six to ten years depending on the discipline. In the STEM (science, technology, engineering, and mathematics) subjects, the expectation is that the research project essentially becomes a full-time job. One reason for this expectation is that in most STEM doctoral programs, nearly all students are supported on graduate assistantships (GAs). Thus, work outside the department is highly discouraged or prohibited (see more detail in chapter 3). In addition, since research in STEM disciplines is typically laboratory, field, or community based, it is essential to understand that the research may need to be done at any hour on any day. When we were graduate students, there were times when we needed to complete research and assignments at 2:00 a.m. It is typical for research faculty in all disciplines to put in sixty- to eighty-hour weeks, especially when there are pending deadlines for grants or manuscripts.

There are, of course, programs that are amenable to completing the degree part-time while working full-time jobs (such as those in education and professional fields such as public health), but as stated above, if the degree is a research doctorate, earning the degree will still be based on the completion and approval of the original research project. Although each faculty member manages their students in their own way, it is essential to gauge the work ethic that is expected when you visit the program and meet with prospective faculty. The current graduate students you will be joining are the best source of information. The key is to ask questions and determine if you are willing to commit the time to meet the expectations. Chapter 5 provides a more detailed discussion about balancing life with the commitment to earn the research-based degree.

A key attribute that stands out for the most successful graduate students is a willingness to engage with faculty, ask for help, and use all the resources at their disposal. These students are able to quickly identify what they need, and if they do not know where it is, they will seek out someone who can help them get it. Like Humberto, they find a way. These students also typically make time to attend information sessions and professional development seminars and use these opportunities to network with faculty and administrators who then advocate for them. In short, they realize they cannot possibly do it by themselves and have enough self-confidence to let others help them. These same attributes also define the most successful faculty. Doctoral-granting universities provide a wealth of student support services and resources, and many of these are discussed in detail in chapter 4. What do you know about the resources at the university you wish to attend? What types of resources do you need to be successful? Are you willing to put in the extra effort to find a way to get your work done when it does not seem possible?

Chapter 2 action items

These two exercises will assist you in gaining clarity about why you want to pursue an advanced degree and in creating an end goal (vision) of where it will take you. While these two exercises may appear rather short, they will both require heartfelt honesty to truly help you take control of this next phase of your life.

GRADUATE SCHOOL SELF-ASSESSMENT

Discuss the following with everyone who has a stake in the graduate school experience.

- What is my motivation to attend graduate school?
- Am I choosing a research doctoral program as my first option?
- What do I want to accomplish in my career?
- What research areas truly inspire me?
- Do I have geographical, work, or personal considerations that need to be addressed?
- What are my financial assumptions and projections?
- How much time am I willing to invest?

VISIONING EXERCISE

- How would you describe your ideal career ten years from now?
- How do you define career success?
- Are/were you achieving some level of career success in your current/previous job? If so, to what do you attribute the success?
- What would you like people to say about you at your sixty-fifth birthday party?
- Who are the people you most admire? What are the aspects of their careers/lives that you would like to emulate?
- How do you prefer to spend your free time?

Three

Is a research doctoral degree a good investment?

Three

IS A RESEARCH DOCTORAL DEGREE
A GOOD INVESTMENT?

Introduction

The answer to the question "Is a research doctoral degree a good investment?" can be tricky and dependent on whom you ask. One thing is certain: completion of a doctoral degree requires a significant investment of time and financial sacrifice. Therefore, it is important that you research the decision to earn an advanced degree from perspectives of cost and return on investment to fully understand how the decision will affect your current and future financial situation.

To help you begin, the first two pieces of information to consider are (1) employment rates for those with advanced degrees and (2) earning potential compared to those who do not have an advanced degree. The most recent statistics from the Department of Labor indicate that individuals who hold master's or doctoral degrees have on average 1.5 to 3 percent lower unemployment rates when compared to those who hold the bachelor's degree. This is certainly good news, but these statistics are aggregates of all disciplines, and since the overall unemployment rate for individuals with advanced degrees is not 0 percent, it means there are individuals with advanced degrees who are unemployed. The data on earning potential show that on average a master's degree will provide about 20 percent higher earnings than a bachelor's degree, and an individual with a research doctoral degree will earn about 50 percent higher earnings than someone with a bachelor's degree. Thus, the potential return on investment for these degrees appears to be very high. However, an important disclaimer to these data is that earnings statistics provide no guarantees of employment.

It is also critical to understand that a research-based doctoral degree (e.g., PhD, EdD) is very different from a professional doctoral degree (e.g., MD, DVM, DPH) when it comes to career trajectory and the credentials for job competitiveness and career development. Professional doctoral degrees are earned through mastery of coursework, demonstrated competency in practicum/internship experiences, and a passing score on a standardized competency exam specific to the discipline that certifies the individual to enter a somewhat-defined pathway to a career in that field. Although the PhD is the terminal degree in most disciplines, there are currently no national competency exams, and the quality and validation of the PhD degree are based on the perceived rigor of discipline-specific outcomes that occurred during the degree program (course mastery, research publication and funding, teaching effectiveness, performances, etc.). Thus, two individuals earning a PhD from the *same* department in the *same* university may have vastly different career prospects due to significant differences in their productivity. To state it simply, the degree itself may qualify you to apply for various positions, but what was accomplished *during the degree program and subsequent postdoctoral training* will enhance your competiveness against the other fifty thousand students who earned the PhD in the year you graduated.

The main purpose of this book is to provide you with sound information and advice that can assist you in planning as you work through your decision process. In this chapter, we will explore various factors that will affect your return on investment (ROI) of earning an advanced degree. We will explore the following elements:

- Cost of attendance—This includes tuition and fees, books, and other supplies.
- Earning potential—This includes an estimation of compensation when you enter the workforce after earning your degree.

- Debt—This includes loans and other debt that will accumulate while you work to complete your program.
- Opportunity costs—This refers to the intangible financial impact of spending your time as a doctoral student instead of being employed full-time.

Cost of attendance. When considering the total cost of attendance (COA), you should include several variables. The Council of Graduate Schools has reported on financial issues affecting graduate students and defines COA as including tuition and fees, books, supplies, room and board, transportation, and personal expenses. The COA will, of course, vary depending on the type of institution you are attending and your field of study. For example, the COA at a university with very high research activity is on average 25 percent higher than the cost to attend other research universities, and the cost to attend a private university can be 50 percent more than if you attend a public university. In addition, the cost to pursue a degree in the social sciences is slightly more than for degrees in the hard sciences and engineering. The table below shows the annual COA for different types of universities and degree programs and the COA as the percentage of income. The second column represents the total income of the student (and spouse if married) in the previous year. You can see that there is very little margin between cost and income.

Table 1: Average Annual Cost of Attendance (COA)

	Average total COA	Average COA as % of income
First-year full-time doctoral students	$48,160	90.80%
Very high research universities	$51,310	93.80%
Research universities	$40,280	86.00%
Public universities	$40,728	90.40%
Private universities	$60,567	93.40%
Science, engineering, and math	$48,959	94.00%
Psychology and other social science	$54,047	94.30%

Source: US Department of Education, National Center for Education Statistics, 2011–12 National Postsecondary Student Aid Study (NPSAS:12)

Earning potential. It is fairly easy to estimate your earning potential as a faculty member. The College and University Professional Association for Human Resources (CUPA-HR) conducts annual salary surveys for faculty positions and other professional positions in the higher-education industry. Executive summaries of the survey results are available on their website (www.cupahr.org) for free. The highest-paying fields for new assistant professors are typically business (and related fields), legal professions and studies, and engineering. Conversely, the fields that tend to pay their new assistant professors the lowest salaries include communication technologies, liberal arts and sciences and humanities, and English language and literature. The Chronicle of Higher Education also has a full faculty salary database that can be accessed through its website.

Debt. About half of doctoral students borrow money to finance their education. Rising debt levels can deter students from pursuing a degree or force them to drop out in the middle of the process. Before taking on loans, make sure that you have explored all possible sources of financial assistance. The graduate school and program director at your institution are good places to start. Students who manage their debt wisely are better situated to complete their degrees and move on to pursue career opportunities.

The level of debt you incur will vary depending on the institution you choose and your academic discipline. Doctoral recipients in the social sciences, education, and the humanities tend to graduate with about twice the debt as those who receive doctorates in the hard sciences and engineering. The reason for this discrepancy is that there is a high proportion of faculty within the hard sciences and engineering who obtain funding to support their research program and can provide graduate assistant research stipends to their students. The hard sciences and engineering also offer numerous laboratory courses at the undergraduate level, and many graduate students in these disciplines can reduce their COA by working as teaching assistants. The social sciences, education, and the humanities also offer teaching assistantships, but in many cases, there are fewer in these disciplines, and they may be offered to more senior-level students. Additional details about these support mechanisms are provided in the sections below.

Opportunity costs. Anyone who has studied economics is familiar with the concept of opportunity cost. Opportunity cost identifies what you give up or sacrifice to pursue a given course of action. For example, if you choose to spend your money on a vacation instead of putting it in your savings account, the interest that you do not reap is an opportunity cost of the vacation.

There is ongoing national discussion about student debt and the time it takes to earn a degree. You might ask why this topic is so important and why there would be strong opinions about the time it will take to earn a graduate degree. It's your life, right? If you need more time, so what? The old saying "Time is money" could not be more true when it comes to completing a degree. The reality is that delays in earning any type of degree push back your point of transition into the labor market. In other words, every semester you spend working on your degree is a semester without a job that will potentially pay you considerably more than what you are making while in school (possibly on a graduate stipend, for example). If you are paying the full costs to earn the degree, your debt will increase each year you spend in school, and this is compounded by the fact that this will be one less year that you are in the market. Even if you are working full-time while pursuing your degree, you will have less earning potential than when after you complete the degree (see the data presented earlier).

To illustrate this point, let's use the example of Gwen, a psychology student. According to table 2 below, Gwen's cost of attendance is $54,047 per year. This includes tuition and fees, books, supplies, room and board, transportation, and personal expenses. The data in table 1 indicate that Gwen's COA is 94.3 percent of her income. Therefore, Gwen's annual income as a graduate student is estimated at $57,314. Table 2 points out that tuition, fees, books, and other expenses directly related to her student status make up 60 percent of the cost of attendance, which equals $32,428.

Table 2

Expenses	Student	Employee
Tuition, fees, books, etc.	$32,428	$0
Room and board, transportation, and personal expenses	$21,619	$21,619
Total expenses	$54,047	$21,619

Now let's look at the changes to Gwen's income once she graduates. As we mentioned above, Gwen's income as a graduate student is estimated at

$57,314. According to CUPA-HR's 2013 salary survey for faculty, the starting salary for a new assistant professor at a research university is $66,816.

Table 3

Income	Student	Employee
Graduate assistantship, fellowship, etc.	$57,314	$0
Annual salary	$0	$66,816
Total income	$57,314	$66,816
Less expenses	($54,047)	($21,619)
Net income	$3,267	$45,197

From this information it should be clear that the earlier you graduate, the lower your opportunity costs will be and the earlier you will realize a return on your investment. Each year graduation is delayed, the $45,197 of net income is delayed, which adds to the opportunity cost for that delayed year. Obviously, this is an elementary exercise to demonstrate a point and does not include many additional factors that affect a person's budget, such as taxes. This example also does not account for the fringe benefits that are offered to college and university employees, including contributions to retirement. Employer retirement contributions can be between 5 and 10 percent of your annual base salary. For Gwen, this would result in an additional $3,340 to $6,681 per year. Assuming those funds are invested in a mutual fund that yields on average 7 percent per year, in twenty years that single-year contribution would add between $13,000 and $26,000 toward Gwen's nest egg.

Another way to place the impact of opportunity costs in perspective is to consider the situation for students who do not complete the degree. Each semester you invest in a doctoral program is significant. If you are struggling to complete your degree, then go through the exercise of calculating the potential financial cost to you each semester your graduation is delayed. That knowledge might help light a fire under you and help you better assess priorities for your time and energy. It is also important to realize that leaving the program after investing several years could be a significant hit to your financial well-being. This is why there is so much riding on your decision to earn a research doctoral degree and so much concern by national leaders about the ~60 percent completion rate in doctoral programs.

A final point to consider is that, historically, many individuals enter graduate school when there is a recession in the economy. If you have been laid off or are in a job with limited career potential, then the opportunity cost of pursuing a graduate degree would be less, and it can make a lot of sense to take advantage of the slow economy to invest in additional credentials. This can be a smart hedge on preparing yourself to be more marketable once the economy improves. However, some students have found themselves on the wrong side of a recession, finishing their degrees during a poor economic environment and waiting years to get a job in the field. While it is impossible to predict the future, recognizing opportunity costs can help you make an informed decision about the best time to attend graduate school.

How can I get financial assistance?

A few points of clarification need to be offered before we begin a discussion about financial assistance. First, if you are pursuing a master's degree, the opportunities to obtain university support (graduate assistantships or fellowships) are very limited at most major research institutions. This is because most master's programs, especially those that do not require original research, typically generate large amounts of tuition for the university. Although there may be potential scholarships available for these types of programs, you need to enter into them knowing that in the majority of cases the bulk of the cost will be yours. Second, the number of doctoral degrees awarded by an institution is a credential to the prestige of the university. Thus, doctoral programs are a major asset to the university, and because of this, the university invests funds in academic programs in the form of full tuition and moderate stipends that leverage the costs associated with obtaining the research doctorate (e.g., PhD, EdD).

According to the National Center for Education Statistics National Postsecondary Student Aid Study (NPSAS), 85 percent of students in PhD programs (except in education) receive some type of financial aid during their programs of study. The type of aid varies, but 68 percent comes from the university itself in the form of institutional fellowships, scholarships, tuition waivers, and employee support. In addition, nearly 58 percent of students in PhD programs (except in education) report they were awarded some type of graduate assistantship (9.6 percent in education). Only 17.3 percent of PhD students support their education through loans, compared to greater than 81 percent of the students in MD and other professional doctoral programs. This large difference in university-supported aid to the students in research doctoral programs exists because the universities benefit from the teaching and research productivity these students provide. Finally, to earn the PhD and generate the productivity outcomes discussed earlier (especially those in STEM disciplines), a full-time commitment that usually involves greater than forty hours of research effort per week is required.

Due to the duration and cost of earning the research doctoral degree, it is essential to investigate and understand all the options that exist for financial assistance. The majority of graduate students indicate that financial support is the main determining factor in their ability to complete their respective programs. Students employed outside their universities in positions that are not connected to their research or degree programs, even part-time, tend to complete their degrees later than they otherwise would. Thus, it is essential to know the financial commitment of your specific department at the start of your doctoral journey so you don't spend precious time stressing about how you are going to finance and finish your degree. Your letter of acceptance should specifically address the form, amount, and duration of any financial commitment to you. If this is not provided, you need to ask for it in writing.

The university's graduate school will be the best resource to get information on the policies regarding financial assistance. The graduate program director in your academic department will also be able to provide information on how you can apply for graduate assistantships and other financial opportunities. The desired situation is, of course, to be funded for your studies so outside employment is not necessary. It should be obvious that if the degree is based on completing an original research project, the more time you can spend on the research, the faster you will be able to complete it. Remember that the completion, and in many cases peer-reviewed publication, of the original research project to the satisfaction of your major professor and dissertation committee is the determining factor in earning the PhD degree. In the following sections, we will explore the various funding mechanisms.

Graduate assistantships (GAs). "Graduate assistantships" is the catchall term used to describe several different employment opportunities typically available to students pursuing a PhD degree at research-intensive universities. The GA is typically considered employment by the university because it provides a service to the university in the form of teaching and research support to the faculty. In most cases, students who receive a GA get a full or partial tuition waiver and a stipend for the duties they are providing. The amount of the stipend is dependent on the funding source, discipline, and duties. For the most recent national data, consult the annual *Oklahoma State Graduate Assistant Stipend Survey.* Most GAs require a ten- to twenty-hour-per-week commitment over one semester or a full year. GAs are usually awarded each academic year, and in many cases, departments have a limit on how many years a student may be supported if the funds are coming from the university. Typically, doctoral students within most STEM disciplines are fully supported by GAs. For non-STEM disciplines it is essential to recognize whether the department has funds for GA appointments and how awards are determined. Descriptions of the types of GAs and the standard commitments and duties are provided below.

Teaching assistantships (TAs). The TA assignment is generally in support of undergraduate teaching during the fall, spring, or summer semesters. The type of duties required for a TA may entail any of the following: (1) assisting faculty with a large course by helping with course management, grading, and office hours; (2) prepping all the laboratory sections for a specific course; (3) serving as the instructor for one or two laboratory sections; (4) developing the curriculum and serving as the instructor for an introductory course; or (5) serving as the facilitator for several recitation/breakout sessions in support of a course. It is important to understand that TA assignments do not all have the same duties, and your eligibility for a TA may be based on the amount of postbaccalaureate coursework you have completed and your level of English-language competency. As you gain more experience as a TA, additional higher-level teaching assignments may also be available depending on your discipline. The number of TAs within a given department is typically based on the number of undergraduate laboratories or introductory course sections the department offers. For example, in a large research university, the departments of chemistry, biology, math (STEM disciplines), and English often have a high number of TA positions assigned to them because they must schedule many different sections of labs and introductory courses to serve students across multiple disciplines.

> *Peter was in my office for the third time to complain about his teaching assistantship. "How does he expect me to manage my lab sections and put in fifty hours of bench research each week? I have to keep up with the grading, and I thought I was allotted twenty hours to devote to my TA each week." Peter was a third-year student in the physics department and was voicing a major complaint I had heard from STEM doctoral students for many years. The challenge for these students was trying to balance their teaching assignment and the expectation of their major professor that they spend every moment in the laboratory.*

A critical point to remember about having a TA assignment is that these positions (especially in STEM disciplines) are in some cases perceived to take time away from the students' bench research. As mentioned previously, most doctoral students are pursuing their degree full-time, and this means at minimum a forty-hour work week. So if you are awarded twenty hours per week as a TA, then that may result in a sixty-hour work week, and it will be critical to have balance between your research and teaching. As noted in the story of Peter, some research faculty have difficulty appreciating the demands on a student who is managing both a TA assignment and their research project.

> *Vivekka saw me at graduation and was smiling ear to ear. She had just been conferred her PhD in cell biology and had accepted a position as an assistant professor at a small private liberal arts college. "I really appreciate*

your help and support," she said as she shook my hand. "I don't think I would have been as competitive if you had not encouraged me to take the teaching workshops offered through the Teaching and Learning Center. The recommendation from the director was also a plus, I think." It was great to see such a positive outcome, but much of the credit for the happy ending is due to the support provided by Vivekka's major professor, who encouraged her to explore that career option and allowed her time to develop her teaching and take advantage of the university resources in that area.

The good news for students like Peter and Vivekka is that many universities are putting greater efforts into professional development training in teaching for doctoral students. Although it would seem natural that students would be provided training, it is unfortunate that many students can be assigned TA positions without a high level of instruction and guidance. However, if you do your due diligence and research your department and university as outlined in this book, you will be able to get a good feel for the attitude about TAs and the amount of support the department and university put into professional training. You also must be honest with yourself and your major professor regarding your career plans. If you desire the PhD and are sure you want to become a faculty member at a teaching university, then you will be much more marketable with documented teaching experience and a teaching portfolio. This career goal may not always be compatible with the expectations of your major professor, especially if you are in a STEM discipline, however. As Vivekka demonstrated, it is essential that you have these conversations early.

Research assistantships (RAs). RA positions support funded research projects. Thus, RAs are mostly available to students in STEM fields and other disciplines where faculty have the ability to obtain high levels of research grant funding (such as psychology, anthropology, and some education fields). The money to support the RA (including the stipend, tuition, health care, and other costs) is written into the research grant the faculty submits to a given agency. From a standpoint of research productivity, the RA is the most coveted funding mechanism for a doctoral student, since you are being paid to do the research outlined in the grant, and this will typically encompass your PhD project. However, unlike the TA positions that are funded by the university and represent a recurring cost to support the departmental teaching requirements, the duration of the RA support will depend on the duration of the grant. Most large grants from federal and private organizations are funded to the investigator for three to five years. Thus, unless you are fortunate enough to come into an RA at the beginning of a grant, it is likely that it will end prior to the completion of your PhD. Many faculty deal with this issue by leveraging the funding for their doctoral students, moving them between grants and also rotating students to TA positions if the department has this option. In the disciplines where attainment of extramural funding is a major component of tenure and promotion decisions, it is essential to do your homework and assess the funding history for a potential major professor, especially if they are early in their career.

Graduate assistantships outside the home department. In some instances it may not be possible to receive a TA or RA within your home department; however, there may still be a limited number of GA positions available in other areas of the university that support various administrative functions in strategic university areas. These opportunities are often posted on the university's employment website. These GA positions are typically created by administrative units and employ students across many different disciplines in any number of duties to support the activities of the unit making the hire.

Ramon had one more year to complete his dissertation in community psychology but was not eligible for TA support. His major professor also did not have significant funding to support an RA position. Since Ramon had worked with his major professor in her undergraduate course to create various research projects that interfaced with my office, she contacted me about support for him. I knew Ramon from the class visits I had made and also knew he was well versed in statistical analysis. Since I needed some help with a large STEM persistence project and had a new grant with a GA line, I brought him in to help me out. Through this networking he was able to receive a GA position and much-needed tuition waiver and not only completed his dissertation work but also was coauthor on the article we published on STEM persistence.

The story of Ramon is but one example of the opportunities that may be available to students, and although this story started with an already-established connection, the tutoring and learning center may need assistance with the development of a student-tracking system or with the management of the peer mentors program. They may hire graduate students in several disciplines willing to work in these areas. The larger the institution, the more of these types of positions may be available. These kinds of GA positions are typically funded for nine to twelve months and pay a stipend and tuition like the TA and RA. The one caveat is that these positions are akin to having a job outside your department, and the duties may not always align with your dissertation research. If you pursue these types of positions, it is essential to obtain the approval of your major professor, but in some cases, the approval of your program and graduate director is also required. Most major professors will be happy that you have secured some funding support, but you will clearly need exceptional time-management skills to assure you are satisfying the research requirements of your major professor.

Fellowships. Fellowships are distinct from GAs as they are not employment and are typically considered financial aid. Fellowships may be internal to the university or can come from federal or private entities and are often highly competitive, awarded based on scholarship and merit, and carry a level of prestige for the recipient and the university if awarded from a highly respected national organization. When evaluating the various types of financial support, fellowships might be considered the most desirable because they often provide multiple years of support and allow the recipient to focus exclusively on pursuing and completing their degrees. Most full fellowships prohibit working or teaching during the award (although some fellowships may include a short teaching or internship component to allow for the development of specific competencies in the discipline). Fellowships generally cover tuition and fees in addition to providing a generous stipend.

Most major research universities (and some individual departments) have a program where a limited number of the highest-credentialed incoming doctoral students compete for fellowships that provide full support for up to five years. Usually these awards are not available through individual applications, but each department may nominate one of their top students for consideration. Other fellowships may be available to students only after they reach candidacy or at the time they are writing their dissertations. These may be based on evidence of research productivity. Most graduate school websites have a list of fellowships and scholarships, and it is a good idea to become familiar with the various programs so you or your major professor can advocate for you. Fellowships are also awarded by national organizations and professional societies.

Loans. Although loans are often necessary to provide the financial means to get through your doctoral program, they should be a last resort. We suggest that before signing off on a loan, you exhaust all other means of financial support that have been discussed earlier in this chapter. It is not desirable to enter a job market loaded down with educational debt. Depending on the health of the job market at the time you graduate, you may be competing with thousands of other candidates for a handful of jobs. In addition, if you are in a field where the salary for an assistant professor, or other type of job if you do not go into academia, is relatively low, having a large loan to pay off will add stress to both your own life and that of your family.

If your first-choice school does not offer you as good of a financial assistance package as some other schools, don't hesitate to contact your first choice to negotiate for a better package. Also, if you are already enrolled at a school, you should not be afraid to approach them about receiving a greater amount of assistance.

Many students find themselves in a situation where loans are a necessary income source, so if you find yourself to be one of those students, take comfort in the fact that you are in good company. Finaid.org is a good source of information on various types of financial aid, including loan options. We will briefly describe some of the more common types of loans available to students, including federal student loan programs, parent loans, and private student loans.

Federal student loan programs. The US government offers two types of student loan programs, including the William D. Ford Federal Direct Loan Program and the Federal Perkins Loan Program. The Direct Loan program is the largest federal student-loan program. These loans are called direct loans because the loan comes directly from the US Department of Education. The Perkins Loan Program, for students with exceptional financial need, is a school-based loan program where the school is the lender. For the most up-to-date information about federal student loan programs, you are encouraged to visit the US Department of Education website.

Parent loans. Parent loans are made through the Federal Direct Loan Program, and just as the name implies, parent loans can be taken out by parents of dependent students to supplement financial aid. This program allows parents to borrow money to cover costs not already covered, up to the full cost of attendance. Since parent loans are the financial responsibility of the parent, if the student fails to make payments, the parents are held responsible. Also, starting in 2006, the program began allowing graduate and professional students to directly borrow through a parent loan to pay for their own education.

Private student loans. Private student loans are offered by private lenders, not the government, and eligibility often depends on your credit score. This type of loan is desirable for students who need to supplement other financial income sources or need more flexible repayment options. As you might guess, interest rates for private student loans tend to be higher than government-offered loans, but the rates are typically less than what you would be charged on a credit card. Therefore, it is wise to first exhaust the Stafford Loan and parent loan before looking into a private loan.

EMPLOYER EDUCATION BENEFITS.

Sheila was employed as an academic administrator at a major research university. Although she enjoyed her job and was highly committed to students, she desired to have a higher-level position that required a graduate degree. Unfortunately, one credit hour of graduate tuition was $350, and *she simply could not afford the cost with her salary. She was fortunate to have a great boss who told her that, as an employee of the university, she was eligible to take up to six undergraduate or graduate credit hours per semester. As she did the math, she discovered that this added up to about $20,000 in tuition that she would not have to pay over the course of her program.*

Many employers, particularly large organizations and educational institutions, provide some type of educational benefit to their employees and their dependents. Some are more generous than others, and many require the employees to maintain a certain grade-point average to remain eligible for the benefit. In addition, the employer may require that you remain employed with them for a specified period of time following the completion of the degree. This is a significant investment by the employer, and they want to be able to reap the return on their investment. Eligible expenses typically include tuition, fees, books, supplies, and equipment. In many cases, this type of funding is tax-free up to a certain limit, which is determined by the Internal Revenue Code.

According to the National Postsecondary Student Aid Study (NPSAS), about 20 percent of graduate students receive some level of employer-sponsored educational benefit. The benefit is most commonly used by students in MBA programs. Of course, most students who are able to take advantage of this funding source do so while holding down full-time jobs, unless the benefit is through their parents' employer. Some employers also offer educational leave benefits, which allows employees to take a leave from their jobs for up to one year to pursue educational opportunities. This is fairly rare but worth exploring if you happen to work for such an organization.

How much money will I need?

Developing an annual budget is an important part of your educational experience. It will help you understand your total expenses as well as funding sources you will need to ensure you minimize the chances of a financial crisis during your graduate studies. If you are not experienced with developing a budget, try to find someone you know and trust to help you work through it. While budget development may seem straightforward and intuitive, it can take some practice and tweaking to get yourself to a point where you are confident you can realistically stay within the budget you have set.

If you have been used to living with more resources than you will have as a doctoral student, also develop a plan for which habits you will need to adjust under a tighter budget. If you are used to a daily dose of caramel macchiato from the local coffee shop, that extravagance may no longer be possible within your new budget.

A basic budget will include general categories for both expenses and income. As a graduate student, your expenses will include tuition and fees; books and supplies; housing and meals; health insurance; transportation; and miscellaneous personal expenses such as clothing, entertainment, haircuts, and your occasional coffee shop indulgences. Your income categories may include assistantships, fellowships, grants, tuition waivers, loans, and any other income you may have, such as a part-time job or financial assistance from parents, a spouse, or a partner. It is typical to start with an annual budget and then break it down by month or semester. Below is a sample budget to help you get started.

Table 4: Sample Annual Budget

Expenses		Income	
Tuition and fees	$22,000	Assistantships	$10,000
Books and supplies	$1,500	Fellowships	$15,000
Housing	$8,000	Grants/scholarships	—
Meals	$5,000	Loans	$2,000
Health insurance	$4,000	Tuition waivers	$18,000
Transportation	$1,500	Other	—
Personal expenses	$3,000		
Total expenses	**$45,000**	**Total income**	**$45,000**

If you find that, after estimating all your expenses and income sources, your income is lower than your expenses, then there are basically two approaches to resolve this: either you will need to identify additional sources of income or you will need to find ways to reduce your expenses.

Keep in mind also that accounting for cash flow will likely be different from just averaging your annual expenses over twelve months. Funds you receive from a fellowship or grant may come in one or two payments and may come at the beginning or end of the academic year; however, some of your expenses will be due at different times during the year from when you receive income. It is important to know when you will be receiving your various sources of income and when you need to pay your various expenses so you can make sure you have the funds available to pay the bills when they are due.

It is also wise to consult with a tax expert so you can estimate the amount you will owe in taxes. Your institution's graduate school may have staff on hand who can help you identify professionals who can work with you on financial planning.

Hopefully the topics that have been addressed in this chapter have sparked some thoughts about your own situation. Graduate school is challenging enough without adding the stress of finding yourself in a poor financial situation. If you are unsatisfied with your current financial condition or have not gone through the process of developing a budget, we encourage you to follow the action exercise below.

Chapter 3 action plan

Budgeting exercise. A budget is useful only if it provides an accurate picture of your financial reality. Therefore, before you dive in, it is important that you take time to get organized and ensure you have accurate information regarding your income and expenses. Following these steps will help to ensure you are developing a useful budget.

1. Gather your financial statements, including bank statements, investment and retirement account statements, credit card statements, pay stubs, and any other documents that will help you understand the amount you are spending or earning. If you can, gather statements from across a six-month period so you have a better sense of how much you are spending and earning on average.

2. Record all sources of income. This may include paychecks from a job; interest and dividends from investments; or student-related income such as grants, fellowships, and assistantships.

3. Record your expenses—everything you spend money on. Make a list of the expenses you incur each month, such as rent, car payment, insurance, groceries, utilities, and other items. If you tend to pay for your expenses with a credit or debit card, those statements will provide useful information to help you capture all the regular places where you tend to spend money. Also be sure to record expenses that are not paid monthly so that you incorporate those into your budget. For simplicity's sake, you may wish to divide an annual expense into twelve months to capture it as a monthly expense.

Expenses		Income	
Tuition and fees		Assistantships	
Books and supplies		Fellowships	
Housing		Grants/scholarships	
Meals		Loans	
Health insurance		Tuition waivers	
Transportation		Other	
Personal expenses			
Total expenses		Total income	

4. Total your monthly income and expenses. If your total income exceeds your total expenses, you are in good shape. If your expenses exceed your income, you will need to make some decisions to increase your income, reduce your expenses, or both.

5. Review your budget every month to make sure you are living within the guidelines you have established or to make adjustments if anything has changed.

Four

WHAT DO I KNOW ABOUT MY DOCTORAL PROGRAM AND POTENTIAL MAJOR PROFESSOR (DISSERTATION ADVISOR)?

Four

What do I know about my doctoral program and potential major professor (dissertation advisor)?

Introduction

> *Jordan was a part-time doctoral student well into her second year in the College of Education. I could tell she was experiencing mixed feelings. On the one hand, she was ecstatic as she had just attended a professional development workshop on "Choosing a Research Topic and Faculty Mentor" and could see more clearly what she needed to do. On the other hand, she seemed a bit miffed that she was not aware such workshops had been offered at the university for the many years she had already been attending. "I did not know that these types of workshops were offered," she said to me. "Why don't you make them more visible to students?" "Have you looked over the graduate school's website?" I asked. "Because there is a comprehensive list of all the workshops we offer with registration links. We also send the list out to all graduate program directors each semester. You should have been receiving these e-mails all along."*

W e will admit that when we were students at the university, we did not truly understand the overall structure of the university and its available resources until we entered academic administration and were charged with setting up various professional development initiatives and developing communication plans. Even today we have little doubt that many faculty and students are unaware of the richness of student success resources available at their institutions. The reality is that many research faculty are focused on the tasks at hand within their programs and colleges and rarely venture outside this venue physically or academically. This is partially due to the demands they carry but also because their primary responsibilities do not involve a need to know about university resources. Many doctoral programs have a dedicated graduate program director (typically a faculty member) who does the heavy lifting of administrative functions related to admissions management, professional development, student tracking, and dissertation submission requirements.

Although it was disappointing that Jordan did not know these types of workshops were offered, it was not a surprise. Unfortunately, this situation epitomizes the problem faced by all stakeholders involved in transforming graduate education: How do you communicate the message about what you are doing to ensure it effectively percolates down to faculty and students? This is particularly challenging at large research universities with thousands of graduate faculty and students who often remain siloed in their respective disciplines. Graduate students often must aggressively seek out professional development opportunities.

What university resources are available to assist me in my graduate education?

To be proactive in assuring you do not end up like Jordan, it is essential to invest some effort in understanding what student success resources are available both within and outside your program. Nearly all doctoral-granting institutions have a dedicated graduate school or graduate studies office. These units typically provide professional development workshops over a range of topics such as navigation of graduate school, public speaking, publication, leadership, and presentation. The graduate school may also partner with offices that provide training in teaching and pedagogy. The titles of these offices will vary among institutions, but some common titles include the Center of Teaching and Learning, Academy of Teaching and Learning Excellence, or Center of Professional Development. These offices may offer short workshops and seminars but also structured programs that entail taking courses and completing a teaching project that may qualify you for a certificate to validate your teaching competency. Other important student-support areas to look for include the following:

- Career center
- Library
- Office of Research
- Center for Student Engagement
- Writing center
- Counseling center
- Student Disability Services
- Office of Community Engagement

The exact names of the units may vary across different institutions, but these offices can provide assistance with career counseling, stress management, scholarship and research databases, responsible conduct in research (RCR) training, and assistance with writing. Finally, most universities also have a graduate student organization that serves the general student population as well as discipline-specific organizations that serve students in individual programs. Jordan was not aware of any of these and did not make the connection that these organizations not only provide the ability to network with peers in her program but also can provide access to students across many disciplines, facilitating a network of colleagues who can provide immediate answers and advice on navigating the complex university system. The important point is that if you take a small amount of time to research each of these important resources before entering an institution or shortly after you arrive, then you will be approaching your graduate education from an informed perspective that may shave months or even years off the time to complete your degree. You will also begin to accumulate a list of key faculty, staff, students, and administrators who are engaged in helping you find the resources you need to succeed.

> *The "Demystifying Publication" workshop was scheduled from 5:15 to 6:45 p.m., and twenty graduate students had registered to attend. By 5:25 p.m., only twelve students had arrived, so I started the session. During the workshop, an additional two students arrived. When I returned back to the office after completing the workshop, I sent e-mails to those who were absent to inquire about the reason they had not attended. To my dismay, several responses indicated that the major professor had questioned the students about the time commitment to attend the workshop and its impact on their research progress. When I talked with other students a few days later about why they never registered for the various workshops, I was told they were afraid to attend these sessions because doing so would be perceived as though they were not working hard enough on their research.*

Although you may discover a wealth of resources, the story above highlights the importance of engaging in direct communication with faculty about the value of these events (especially in those fields that place a high value on the time spent at the lab bench). Be assured that graduate administrators spend a great deal of time discussing the value of these types of initiatives with the university stakeholders; however, building this training into the culture of graduate education is still a work in progress at many universities and especially in the STEM disciplines. By addressing questions about accessibility and commitment to resources with faculty during recruiting visits and interviews, you will be able to assess whether a particular university or particular faculty member is committed to providing access to professional development and teaching enhancement for their mentees. These opportunities are becoming especially important for competitiveness if your career aspirations go beyond becoming a research faculty at a major research university. The good news is that professional development of graduate students outside their research disciplines is on the national radar at the Council of Graduate Schools, National

Institutes of Health (NIH), National Science Foundation (NSF), and other key agencies. But if you are a student already engaged in a graduate program and are experiencing problems with accessing resources, initiate a discussion with the graduate student leaders and graduate school administrators about offering remote access to the sessions via the web or podcasts. You will probably find that there are many other students in the same situation, and you may encounter administrators who are willing to advocate to your college and academic program leadership to assure you have access to the resources.

What is a major professor (dissertation advisor)?

All doctoral programs require the dissertation research to be completed under the direction of a major professor (dissertation advisor/mentor) and an advisory committee. The dissertation advisor is usually referred to as a major professor, and we will use this term throughout the chapter. If the research project is interdisciplinary, many programs allow two faculty to serve as co-major professors. It is important to consider that no program actively tries to fail out a percentage of the students it admits. The successful mentoring and graduation of doctoral students is a performance measure for the faculty and university. Each university has defined criteria for the eligibility of faculty to serve as a major professor to doctoral students, and these criteria are usually stipulated in the graduate catalog. If you take the time to review the graduate catalog, you may notice there is not a lot of detail about the actual duties a major professor should perform in this role. The main reason for this is because the day-to-day duties of a major professor are dependent on the individual, the discipline, and the culture of the institution. However, the primary role of the major professor includes (1) advising on academics and assuring that you remain in good academic standing; (2) guiding/mentoring the research project; (3) assuring the research project meets university compliance standards associated with Institutional Review Board (IRB), Institutional Animal Care and Use Committee (IACUC), and so on; (4) assuring you have access to the appropriate resources (and funding) to complete the research; and (5) providing the oversight for the completion and approval of the dissertation.

The list below highlights the attributes of the "perfect" major professor and was compiled from the criteria used to award outstanding graduate mentoring awards from many different universities.

An outstanding major professor (graduate mentor)

- provides defined expectations of performance and helps with training in time management;
- helps with course selection and the timeline for completion;
- discusses general college and university policies related to graduate education—or helps in determining where answers can be found;
- provides an introduction to the literature base and the prominent scholars in the discipline;
- offers guidance in finding ideas for research projects or assistance with developing and focusing the research question;
- provides funding for research and assistance in identifying funding opportunities;
- provides training in appropriate methods of data collection and analysis;
- provides training related to specific research skills and guidance in handling unexpected research findings;
- provides training in writing, speaking, and presentation skills;
- provides opportunities to present and discuss research findings with critical feedback;
- provides opportunities to publish and gives timely review of manuscripts;
- provides opportunities to present research at conferences;
- provides opportunities to teach and support for teaching enhancement;
- provides career counseling and assistance with job placement;
- is always available; and
- is supportive and mentors with affirmation.

It should be obvious that it will be very difficult to identify a single faculty member who embodies all these attributes. The key is that you identify which of these attributes are the most important to you so you can begin having discussions with faculty and identifying departmental environments that provide you the best opportunities to succeed (see the action exercise at the end of this chapter). There are always a few faculty members who believe graduate school is like boot camp, and the doctoral degree should be a symbol not only of scholarly achievement but also of pure raw persistence to overcome unbearable circumstances. Do not succumb to this myth. It is OK to flee from those who want to make you feel as though getting through graduate school should be a torturous process. With that said, a critical point to consider is that the major professor is *not the only person* at the institution who can provide you authentic mentorship! You will find that there are a number of faculty, staff, and administrators who are 100 percent dedicated to your success and will do everything within their power to help you.

What do I know about the faculty research interests in my graduate program?

Most graduate programs have well-developed websites that list all associated faculty, their measures of scholarship, and their roles in the department. It is essential to fully review the research description for all faculty because you will need to identify (1) a potential major professor, (2) two to three other faculty who will serve as members of your dissertation advisory committee, and (3) additional faculty who may serve in other mentorship roles. In your discussions with the faculty, it is imperative that you approach all conversations from the perspective of research and that you have done your homework on their research questions and productivity. You will find that most research faculty welcome engaged discussion from a student who has invested some effort into their research interests, and this can make the difference in getting admitted. The faculty want to invest in those who have the same passion toward research as them and who they believe will see it through.

To get more details regarding faculty scholarship, there are numerous national databases, such as the National Center for Biological Information (NCBI), Google Scholar, ISI Web of Science, Education Resource Information

Center (ERIC), ARTSTOR, and subdiscipline databases that can be searched to assess the publication/creative work record of the faculty. The main institutional library will have access to all these databases and will also assist students in finding the relevant scholarship or discipline-specific databases for a specific faculty member. Many faculty also maintain their own web pages that are full of useful information and may include their CV or provide lists of their current graduate students or postdoctoral scholars. This information can be used to match names to publications (to determine if the faculty is publishing with their students) and to gauge whether the faculty can take on additional students. It is essential to spend the time researching all the faculty within a department to obtain as much information as possible about the scope of research and their level of productivity. Create a profile of each faculty that includes reprints of their most current scholarship, and take this with you to an interview to guide your questions. The more active you make the conversation, the more validation you bring to your commitment.

A common question we get from prospective students concerns the method of communication to faculty and how and when it is appropriate to contact them. The answer is that all prospective doctoral students should attempt to engage with potential mentors (major professors) as early as possible during the admission process. If at all possible, you should meet the faculty members face to face before committing to a program. If you are invited to an on-site interview, be prepared to request meetings with specific faculty whose research interests you. Be prepared to have the formative discussion described earlier about your mutual research interests and to demonstrate your passion for the discipline (and answer the "Why do you want to go to graduate school?" question with a high level of commitment). Note that your admission to a doctoral program is a significant investment of both faculty time and money, and you need to demonstrate why the faculty should make the investment in you and provide evidence that you will complete the program. However, do not lose sight of the fact that you also should be evaluating the faculty member and determining whether this is an individual you could spend the next four to six years working with. If a one-on-one meeting is not possible, send a professionally crafted, brief e-mail of introduction to let the faculty know you have applied to the program and are

interested in their research. Most doctoral programs receive many more qualified applicants than they have slots, so the time spent engaging directly with the
faculty can make the difference in getting admitted to the program.

What is the process for choosing a major professor (dissertation advisor)?

When embarking on a course of study to earn a research doctoral degree, it
is critical to recognize that doctoral education requires you to interact with
faculty much more directly than undergraduate education does. This interaction is the cornerstone to progress and allows you to build relationships as you
progress to becoming a true colleague with the faculty. The one-on-one train-
ing/mentoring is essential to the success of all graduate students, although the
amount of time devoted to this type of interaction varies by discipline.

*Scott sat in my office fuming. "How can someone with such a reputation
in anthropology put no effort into advising us? All we do is work! There
is no personal touch, and he does not care at all that we have our own
lives and responsibilities outside of this institution!" I was well aware of
Professor Barkley, how he ran his research operation, and that he had
greater than a 60 percent attrition rate for doctoral students who started
in his laboratory. I had even assisted in the placement of other promis-
ing students from his program who simply could not work in such an
environment but who excelled when placed with student-centered faculty.
Unfortunately, the concerns that Scott was articulating about Professor
Barkley were similar to those I had heard from other students across many
disciplines at the university. But Professor Barkley was a star in the eyes of
the university president and other high-ranking administrators due to his
national reputation and record of scholarship. If he chewed up and spit
out a few students, so what?*

The great majority of doctoral programs allow you to choose the faculty
member who will serve as your major professor. This makes sense because

the major-professor–doctoral-student relationship cannot be healthy unless both agree that they want to work together. In addition, the professional relationship that is forged during the many-year process of earning the degree cannot be sustained beyond the degree if both parties have not agreed to work together. Thus, we like to equate the choice of the major professor to that of choosing a life partner. Although this statement always gets some laughs when it is used in workshops, it is not meant as a joke. Consider the following similarities between marriage and your doctoral education:

- You will be linked in name with the major professor for life on the title page of the dissertation (and also if the discipline is one in which there will be coauthored publications).
- You will have to interact with your major professor for a period of at least four to five years. (The most current data indicates that marriages last less than eight years!)
- You will need the support and counseling from the major professor as you move forward in your career.
- You may need to rely on the major professor for financial support during your graduate education.
- The best major professors are there to help you pick up the pieces and provide support for education issues as well as those issues that affect your well-being.
- Your major professor can help you meet (network) new people due to their previous associations.

Megan was clearly going to fail her doctoral oral comprehensive exam. She simply was unable to move through the most basic questions and seemed frozen and overwhelmed. As one of her committee members, I tried to give Megan a lifeline with a very simple question I hoped would get her talking and allow her to gain some confidence. She thought about it for a minute but was now so flustered that she was past the point of no return. The committee asked her to leave the room, and then we began to discuss the options we would allow for her to continue in the program. Since I had taught

Megan in my class and knew she was an exceptional researcher, I was quite dismayed by her performance and asked her major professor how he had helped her prepare for this key benchmark. His response still resonates with me fifteen years later. "It was her job to be prepared for this exam, and although she asked me for some guidance, I told her she needed to figure it all out for herself because I had a grant deadline that took priority."

The importance of developing a quality mentoring relationship is a key theme throughout this chapter, and it is important to know that even the best faculty may have many students competing for their time. In our experience, the choice of the major professor is the single most important *decision* that will affect your ability to complete the research doctorate. Studies published by the Council of Graduate Schools (cgsnet.org) and in the Chronicle of Higher Education (chronicle.com) routinely list lack of quality mentorship as one of the top reasons why graduate students do not complete the doctoral degree. In Scott's case, he did not get to know Professor Barkley before deciding to join his research group. Scott said later that he did fully research Professor Barkley's website and based his decision to work with him on his national reputation and the number of publications and conference presentations Professor Barkley had produced. What he failed to notice was that few of Professor Barkley's publications had any graduate students listed as secondary authors, that he supported very few students in attending national conferences, and that he was often away from the university giving lectures at other institutions. Before accepting the position to join Professor Barkley's research team, Scott also did not talk to any of the other graduate students about what it was like to work in Professor Barkley's world. Scott's case actually did result in a happy ending because he was able to get into a different research group, produced several fine publications, and ultimately earned his PhD. He is now a faculty member at a small liberal arts college and fully enjoys collegial interaction with his undergraduate students. On the other hand, Megan found herself in a situation where the faculty member was highly productive but poorly trained regarding mentorship and oversight of students. In both cases, the breakdown was at the level of the mentoring relationship.

So what is the solution to improving mentoring, and how should you approach the process as you consider your options for a major professor? The first step for you is to identify the most important attributes you need in the research mentoring relationship. As stated earlier, it is important to recognize that the major professor will be the individual who is involved in the primary oversight of your research project. A mentorship self-assessment is provided at the end of this chapter to assist you in determining the type of mentoring you need. Once you complete the self-assessment, the next step is to identify a potential major professor who can provide the mentoring relationship you have identified.

If you are admitted to a program *prior* to choosing a major professor, there are many ways to obtain information about potential mentors. If you have taken courses with faculty during your graduate program, you can refer to your observations of how they interacted with students in class and your personal interactions with them to assess their suitability to serve as your major professor and meet your mentoring needs. In addition, your engagement with individual faculty in these settings may be critical in establishing a relationship that could make the difference if you end up competing with another student for that faculty member. It is also important to speak with other graduate students in the program, especially those who have been at the university for a number of years. Finally, the graduate program director can also provide some insights, but since graduate program directors are likely to be faculty also and potential mentors themselves, they may not be comfortable providing full disclosure about other faculty members in their department.

Finally, some programs require that you identify a faculty member who will commit to you as a "sponsor" of your application (and potential major professor) as a condition of admission to the program. In these instances, the sponsor may serve to advise you during your first few semesters and may evolve into your major professor, or you may have some flexibility to find a different mentor. In either case, you may not have had the faculty teach you prior to making a decision about their compatibility to your mentoring needs. Therefore, there is increased importance on completing a thorough review of the faculty's research records, contacting current graduate students via e-mail or phone, and visiting the program to meet with faculty as discussed earlier. Regardless of which situation you encounter, the process must be an active one on your part. Always remember that as a research doctoral student, your success is collateral for the department, major professor, and university.

What are the expectations for the development of my research project?

Before the incident reached my desk, Jose had already sent letters to the president and provost demanding that justice be done. He had completed all of his coursework and simply wanted to schedule his thesis defense. His program had refused. The problem was that he had never set up a thesis advisory committee or identified a major professor and had simply completed the research on his own with no faculty oversight. A review of the work revealed that it lacked a graduate-level research question, was poorly written, and also was not in an area that overlapped with the faculty in the department. I met with Jose and advised him that he had not followed graduate policy or the department guidelines and would need to identify a major professor, establish a thesis advisory committee, and defend the research before he could graduate. Jose indicated that this was not how it had worked at his previous institution and insisted that he was not going to change anything because he knew the work better than any of the faculty and did not need their approval. Although I tried to broker a solution, his attitude was so acrimonious that no faculty could work with him. He ultimately left the university.

Do you have to develop a research project before you enter a PhD or thesis-master's program? This question was always asked at the "Developing Your Research Project" workshops. The answer is not straightforward, but there are some overarching expectations to the research project that apply to all disciplines: (1) all disciplines require a major professor to serve as a research mentor (something that Jose failed to recognize); (2) all disciplines require an advisory committee to review the quality of the work and assess progress; and (3) whether you develop the project from scratch or as part of a larger funded project, it is developed through an ongoing iterative process with your major professor. This last point is a key one and something that Jose failed to do. Thus, he failed to establish a relationship with a faculty mentor who was invested in the project and could provide critical oversight to the development and assure that it met the rigors of the discipline. Guidance on the *process* of selecting and developing a research project is provided in chapter 5, but it is important to understand that the expectations regarding how the research project is initiated, developed, and implemented are specific to the discipline and dependent on the philosophy of the major professor. The information below is a general guide to how each discipline handles the development of the research project and is intended to provide some talking points as you research potential departments and engage in discussions with potential mentors.

STEM disciplines. In the majority of STEM disciplines, a significant amount of the research is funded through extramural grants. Therefore, if you desire to work with a particular faculty member, you will likely be working on a piece of their funded project. In these instances, you are typically not responsible for the conception of the project but will have a role in its development and implementation. Therefore, you must be engaged and interested in the same research area as your potential major professor. This does not mean that the process is not iterative and you will not have a creative influence on the research, because as the research evolves, you will be involved in the interpretation of the results and the development of hypotheses that address the next series of questions. This type of model is driven by the fact that (1) the research may be expensive, and a project that is different from the one funded simply cannot be supported by a faculty member in the majority of the STEM disciplines; (2) many STEM doctoral students are entering the doctoral program straight out of a bachelor's program, and their research skills still require significant development; (3) there is usually a very deep technical literature base that must be learned before an original project can be proposed; (4) there are technical skills that must be mastered; and (5) the currency for the faculty (and student) to obtain additional extramural funding is the publication of results derived directly from the funded project. Therefore, it is essential that you fully research each faculty member in the department and gain a full understanding of their research so you can determine if there are specific areas that interest you. In these disciplines, it is also important to determine whether a potential major professor is accepting students.

Health and professional. Much like the STEM disciplines, many of the health fields that award a PhD degree (e.g., medicine, public health, and nursing) carry out research that is extramurally funded. Therefore, if you desire to work with a particular faculty member, you will likely be working on a piece of their funded project. This does not mean you cannot bring experience from previous research projects into your program, but there will need to be a tangible connection to the research you want to do and the research that is carried out by your potential major professor. It is also important to note that just as in the STEM disciplines, there are many cases where the faculty is at capacity and cannot support additional students in their research program.

Humanities. Most humanities disciplines require a master's degree for admission into the doctoral program. Thus, there is an expectation that you will have carried out previous research, written a master's thesis, and potentially published results from the research. In these disciplines, the major professor is not responsible for identifying and setting up the research project; instead, you are expected to take an active role in the project's conception, development, and implementation. Typically, when the dissertation research has developed to a point where an outline of the dissertation can be conceptualized, you will develop a proposal/prospectus with the guidance of your major professor. Due to the broad range of research that can be carried out in the humanities, your major professor may not conduct research in the same area you have chosen. Thus, it is critical to evaluate the interests of the faculty to assure you will be able to engage someone who has the expertise and research interests compatible with your project.

Social sciences and education. The social sciences and education disciplines have multiple models for developing the dissertation project, because faculty are working on both funded and unfunded research projects. However, unlike the STEM disciplines, where you might engage in research rotations in the first semester, social science and education programs typically require a much higher course load that allows you to engage with the faculty and develop relationships before having to make formal decisions about the dissertation project. Social science and education programs also typically admit students to the doctoral program only after they have earned a master's degree, so you may have already engaged in the development, implementation, and completion of a research project that can be further expanded to a dissertation project. If this is the case, it is important to assure there are faculty who have interest in the project and expertise to serve as your major professor. If you are planning to work with a faculty member who already has a funded project, it is essential to discuss your expectation for the development of your dissertation project and whether they are accepting students to come in and work on it.

The arts. In the arts, you are expected to take an active role in the conception of the dissertation project and will work closely with your major professor on the development of a research proposal. As in the other disciplines described above, it is important to assure there are faculty members within the department who match your research interests and have the expertise to serve as a major professor and guide your progress.

Strategies to identify a research topic. If you are in a field where you are primarily responsible for identifying the research question and topic area, an effective strategy to hone in on a research topic for your dissertation is to review the literature related to topics of interest to you. Reviewing the existing literature, particularly recent publications, will enlighten you about theoretical constructs and models, which research questions have been studied, what questions remain for exploration, and how to write for an academic publication. Early in your exploration of research topics, you may have a broad variety of potential topics you are considering for your dissertation. As you progress through your coursework and become more and more exposed to focused research areas in your field, talk to the faculty about topics that interest you. Each semester, work to narrow the focus of your research question. By the time you complete your coursework, you should have a fairly good idea of what you want to study. At that point, your review of the literature should be focused on publications that will help you construct a well-developed litera-ture review for your research proposal.

How does the program certify me for doctoral candidacy?

Most doctoral programs have two distinct parts. The first covers the entry-level period (one to three years depending on the discipline) where you are enrolled in core courses, are engaged in discussions with faculty who may serve as your major professor, and are developing your research project. Depending on the discipline, the coursework may be the predominant activity in the first few years. For example, students in STEM disciplines may have to complete only three to five courses in the first few semesters while also engaged in re-search. In non-STEM disciplines, the course load can be significantly more extensive, with the research activity commencing only after a full proposal has been approved. Typically, once the necessary coursework is completed, most programs require successful completion of several examinations that certify the student to engage in independent dissertation research. Students who suc-cessfully complete the examinations are typically classified as "doctoral can-didates." In some institutions, this classification can also result in reduced tuition costs and reductions in the total number of credits required to remain in full-time status. (However, never equate enrollment in nine hours of dis-sertation research with having a similar hourly work requirement!)

There is no universal structure to the format of the examination to reach candidacy, and each university and discipline has different methods that test a student's competency to stay in the program. Most examinations have both a written and oral component that must be completed within a given time from the original date of enrollment in the program. The written portion can range from a series of closed-book questions that are completed over a number of days to the development of a full-scale research grant (typically in an area that is not related to the dissertation research project) that is submitted to a faculty review committee. The oral portion of the exam usually follows the successful completion of the written portion and can range from questions from the advisory committee on any topic within the general discipline to an oral defense of the full dissertation research proposal. Given the breadth of different examinations, it is wise to review the graduate catalog for the general guidelines the university has established as well as the structure of the examinations within your specific department/program. It may be that one program requires examinations that fit your skills better than another.

Rick applied to many different PhD programs and was fortunate to obtain admission to several universities that each had excellent research faculty and met many of his other criteria. As he went through the process of deciding where to go, one factor that swayed his decision was the examination process. Rick saw great value in being evaluated on his ability to write a grant proposal compared to answering basic questions on material he had already mastered through his general coursework. He also knew that writing research grants was a key requirement of being a successful faculty member in biology, and he viewed the prospect of writing the proposal as a true validation of his ability to develop a research project. When Rick secured his first faculty position, he used portions of that first grant proposal and was able to apply the critical feedback received from the committee to the first grant he submitted as a junior faculty member.

The bottom line is that many students enter a PhD program never having evaluated the process they will need to go through to become a doctoral candidate. This is not a good recipe for success and can catch even the best students by surprise when benchmarks arrive for which they have not prepared. The students who have the best success in graduate school are those who can manage their time and are also proactive at planning to meet key benchmarks.

Chapter 4 action items

Steve Jobs once said, "People don't know what they want until you show it to them." The two exercises below provide a practical approach to helping you see what it is you want in a mentoring relationship. As with the other exercises that accompany each chapter, these take some time and honest thought to produce an outcome that will benefit you. To help you get started, close your eyes, and consider a situation in your life where you achieved a goal that was facilitated with the help of another individual or the attributes of the best boss you have had. What about these experiences resulted in the positive outcomes?

MENTORSHIP SELF-ASSESSMENT.

- *What type of oversight do you need to be the most productive?* Let's face it: doctoral research is a challenge and not full of affirmation. Many research studies may not work, do not give you the results you expect, take longer than anticipated, and need to be repeated over and over. Do you need someone who will keep after you, or do you need someone who will let you work it out? Do you work better if you have defined deadlines or a more open-ended schedule? Can you handle the major professor being out of the country for long periods of time?

- *Do you prefer to work independently or collaboratively?* If you are required to rely on others for data or work as a group, can you do it? Can you productively work independently off campus?

- *Can you work with a mentor who has many other students?* It is likely that the major professor you choose will also be mentoring other individuals (students, staff, postdoctoral scholars). How will you assure you have access to the mentor? What does the mentor do to assure students receive enough oversight?

- *How do you handle criticism?* Being in a doctoral program is an academic and personal growth experience that will have many ups and downs. At its core, research is carried out and presented so it can be critiqued and validated. Can you accept criticism of the research approach or its analysis without feeling it is personal?

- *What is your work ethic?* In some disciplines it is typical for the faculty to work seventy to eighty hours per week. In some instances it may be necessary for you to do the same. Does your work ethic match the expectation of your major professor? Is the discipline you are going into conducive to your current lifestyle? Do you expect flexibility from your mentor and program regarding any family obligations?

- *Do you need the personal touch?* Major professors have very different styles in how they manage and interact with their research group. Are you the most productive in a social environment that builds community by promoting engagement outside the research setting? Do you need a major professor who is interested in talking about nonresearch topics (such as sports, movies, music)?

GUIDING QUESTIONS FOR CHOOSING A MAJOR PROFESSOR.

- *What is the faculty member's current commitment to other students or postdoctoral scholars?* It is essential that you know the current commitments of a potential major professor as this will affect your access to them.

- *How long has the faculty member been at the institution, and what is their rank?* It is important to understand the distinction between an assistant, associate, and full professor. Although it is unfair to judge an assistant professor who has just been hired, how will you feel if four years from now they do not get tenure and you must find a new mentor? In these instances, you need to do your homework and assess the potential of the junior faculty member for success. This can be a very good situation because the faculty will be highly motivated; however, a new assistant professor has also got huge pressures to simply get up and going and may need to spend a great deal of time developing their teaching materials and submitting grants. This may affect their ability to provide the quality mentoring outlined above. Remember that you are a consumer, and you need to shop for the best opportunity that will provide for your success.

- *What is their record of publication/creative works/funding?* To assess a faculty member's research, review the departmental website, which should list their research and scholarship. Many faculty also maintain a research website that may list current students and postdoctoral scholars. If the faculty member does not have a comprehensive CV available, search for scholarship through national databases specific to the discipline. The university library may also have information.

- *How many students have they graduated? How many have left without graduating?* Associate professors and full professors should have mentored students who have completed the degree. In many cases, these students are listed on their CV or website. You can research these students to determine where they are. Senior graduate students in the program may be able to provide information regarding the students who started with the faculty member but did not complete the degree.
- *What is their mentorship style?* If the mentorship style is not obvious from discussions with the faculty member, you may be able to get information from other faculty and current students. There may also be websites (Rate My Professors) that provide insight into how they engage with others. It is critical that they match the key mentoring criteria you identified in self-assessment.
- *Are they supportive of nontraditional students? Do they have a family?* It is critical to assure that a potential mentor is flexible to your needs if you are a part-time student, have family obligations that will impact the time you can commit to being on-site at the university, or have a long commute. You are wise to discuss these items up front with a potential major professor to avoid any misunderstandings. Other faculty and students may be helpful in determining how the faculty member has dealt with these types of situations in the past.

Five

WHAT ELSE CAN I DO TO IMPROVE MY CHANCES OF COMPLETING MY DEGREE?

Five

WHAT ELSE CAN I DO TO IMPROVE MY CHANCES OF COMPLETING MY DEGREE?

Introduction

Throughout the previous chapters, a key message is that earning a graduate degree is one of the most rewarding commitments you can make and requires absolute dedication, time, and sacrifice. Since the average time to earn a doctoral degree is eight years, it should also come as no surprise that there will inevitably be moments of frustration that challenge your stamina and cause you to question your decision. Even if you have a great deal of passion, if you do not possess (or develop) strong self-discipline and a healthy work ethic, meaningful progress and success will be hard to come by. Another consideration to understand about graduate degree progression is that real life is ongoing. As with any process that takes years to complete, the pressures of real life will have an influence on your progress from time to time. Finally, your commitment to the degree will also affect many more people than you may think.

What lifestyle changes will I have to make?

Many students who enroll in a doctoral program have unrealistic perceptions about the lifestyle sacrifices they will have to make to be successful as a graduate student. We have encountered many students who enter a doctoral program thinking the timeline to completion and the workload will be fairly similar to their undergraduate or master's degree program. But as has been discussed in previous chapters, the progression to a doctoral degree is vastly different from an undergraduate or even master's program (especially if the master's degree did not require a research thesis). For students who do not complete the doctoral degree, particularly those who leave after the first year, the decision to leave the program is frequently connected to the realization that the lifestyle of a doctoral student was not what they expected, particularly when measuring it against other goals like having a family and living a more balanced life. This is one reason why only about one percent of the population has a doctoral degree. If you are already involved in a graduate program, you may have already come to the realization that completing the degree requirements will require dramatic changes in your lifestyle.

It was Holly's husband who encouraged her to pursue a doctoral degree. She worked at a university, so she had some level of understanding of graduate student life, and she received further encouragement from deans and other administrators, but it was her husband's prompting that ultimately pushed her forward. Holly's husband was not an academic himself and did not have a graduate degree, so when, after earning her master's degree and having their second child, he suggested that she get a PhD, she wanted to make sure they both understood what that would mean and how it would impact their lifestyle and their marriage. She wanted him to know that she would need to invest significant time and energy to complete the research and move the project forward and that this decision would impact the time she could spend with the family.

If you have family members or other people in your life who will be affected by your decision, it is important to engage in an honest conversation with them about how the decision will change your lives and jointly complete the various action exercises that have been provided in the previous chapters. If you are not sure how your lives will be affected, speak with faculty and fellow students in the program. Along with choosing your major professor, these are some of the most important conversations that will impact your success. Even if you truly know why you want to pursue the degree but the people closest to you don't understand your reasons, or they don't understand the investment and sacrifice needed to finish, you will face a much more difficult road to completion.

> *The weekend was just like every other for the past several months. Tina worked a full-time job during the week, so weekends were her opportunity to make progress on her dissertation in the adult education program. Saturday morning, as usual, she was in front of the computer while her husband was getting things done around the house. Jerry couldn't be more supportive of Tina's desire to pursue her doctorate and always picked up the extra load with the house and the kids so she could focus on her writing. However, Tina couldn't help but be distracted by the sound of her young children playing down the hall and their occasional visits to ask if she would play with them.*

Like Tina, we both completed our research training while raising young children. With our spouses' support, we were able to find study spaces and get some quiet time at home while they served as gatekeepers with the children. If you must be at home to work on any aspect of the degree, it is important to find a place where you can study without distraction. If you live with others, discuss the options with them. It is important to have those close to you on board and supportive of the place and structure that is ultimately decided. This will be a critical time to acknowledge, for yourself and those closest to you, that there are some things you cannot accomplish until the dissertation is completed.

To make progress with your degree, you must prioritize the demands on your time. Many students leave full-time jobs or put off acquiring full-time jobs to pursue a doctoral degree. You may have a hobby like working on cars, competing in model-airplane events, cruising on your bicycle or motorcycle on the weekends, or scrapbooking. As enjoyable as your hobby is to you, there will be times (especially during the writing of the dissertation) when these activities may need to be scaled back or put on hold. In fact, you can use this sacrifice as an incentive to complete your degree. Remember that the completion of the degree is not the last step but the first step in the next phase of your life. If you are married or otherwise cohabitate with a significant other, discuss how your partner may help with this. Housework can consume an incredible amount of time, between laundry, cooking, cleaning, grocery shopping, and all the other duties of keeping up with life. Ask your significant other to lighten your load with these tasks as much as possible. If you normally dedicate Saturday morning to housecleaning and errands, transfer the time to working on your degree. In the previous story, Tina continued to hold a full-time job and pursue her degree part-time while raising a family. This would have been impossible without the solid support she received from her husband, who was willing to make sacrifices himself.

What can I do to remain motivated and efficient?

Crystal had made it to doctoral candidacy in her sociology program, and I still remember her joy at passing that phase of her program. Unfortunately, a year later, I was signing the paperwork for her to voluntarily withdraw. She told me she had an immediate job prospect that required only the master's degree and that she had simply "lost her way" and motivation once she was required to be the sole driver of the project. It did not help that her major professor had taken a one-year sabbatical and was available to mentor her and provide feedback and encouragement only via e-mail or Skype. She also did not have a strong support base and had not built relationships with faculty outside of her research area. Unfortunately, this type of situation is not uncommon when the student's research project is dissociated from the major professor's main research focus.

Crystal's story highlights the fact that no matter what discipline you choose, your success toward a research degree is fully dependent on your perseverance in answering your research question. Think about it. All research is based on a question you will be seeking to answer or solve. Even with the best methods, best resources, and best minds, the outcomes may not answer the question or may result in even more questions that need to be addressed. In addition, the research process typically moves much slower than anyone can predict and may proceed for many months or years without providing affirmation. Therefore, your ability to be self-motivated and find the positives on a daily basis is an essential attribute that must be developed to stay dedicated to your project.

If you are in a discipline that requires you to work more independently without a research team or defined physical structure (such as a laboratory), there is an additional level of discipline that is needed, especially when the research progress is stalled. Even in the STEM disciplines where a full team of individuals may be working on a specific project in a laboratory setting that promotes interactions, students can become uninspired and disengaged simply due to the nature of research. The good news is that there are a number of approaches you can take to help you remain motivated and help you get through the tough times.

Develop a detailed academic plan. First and foremost, you must always remain connected with your major professor. Even if your research project is not directly connected to their core research, the major professor has a responsibility to mentor you and keep you on track. If you have selected you major professor carefully, as we suggested in chapter 4, you will hopefully have a collaborative relationship from the start. One way to engage a major professor is to work directly with them to develop a comprehensive academic action plan. The more detailed your plan, the better.

When first starting out in the program, you will want to map out courses and set key benchmarks, semester by semester (or quarter by quarter if your institution is set up that way). Become familiar with the courses that are required and when they should be taken. If you can choose from a list of electives, identify which ones are most appropriate for you. For all courses, obtain information from the department as to when each course is offered. Some courses are not offered in all terms, and in some cases, a course may be offered only once a year or every two years. If this is the case, be sure you know when the course will be offered and whether there are prerequisites so you can fit them into your plan. Some programs will require you to submit an academic plan of study during the first year of your program. If this is the case for you, try to get this done as soon as possible. You must consult with your major professor, or if you have not identified one at this stage, the graduate program director or department chair for your program. During this part of the program, there will be a great deal of structure since the faculty and university dictate when classes will be held, when assignments are due, and what the nature of the assignments will be.

Engage your major professor in the development of your research proposal. All research-based graduate degree programs require the development of a research proposal or plan of work. The scale of this document varies between disciplines, as do the expectations of your major professor and dissertation committee regarding its development (see the section on developing the research project in chapter 4). A key nuance of any doctoral program is the transition from the structure of weekly class sessions and assignments with deadlines that help students stay focused to the unstructured work of the research program. Making progress on your dissertation requires a much greater amount of self-discipline than when you are taking courses; therefore the quality and detail of the research proposal will have a huge impact on your timeline.

Although your major professor is committed to your progress, you may find he is not proactively checking in with you to make sure you are staying on track and spending your time wisely. This is especially true in disciplines where your project is more autonomous and you are not working in a research team. Many programs require only an annual meeting with your committee and the submission of a yearly progress report. Thus, it is possible that you could work for months with no communication or feedback on your progress. Your major professor will also be advising multiple students, and thus the responsibility to have discussions about progress may fall squarely on you. This is not a criticism of faculty, merely a dose of reality for you to understand the dramatic shift that happens once courses are completed. Graduation hinges on your ability to complete the research and produce an acceptable dissertation.

However, if the major professor is engaged in the development and implementation of the research plan from the beginning, they will be more invested in the project, increasing your chances to connect with them on a regular basis. Regular planned meetings with your major professor will develop a common understanding and discipline you to make progress.

Keep the end goal in view. Once you have completed your courses and are admitted to candidacy, you have one goal: finish the project and write the dissertation. Let nothing distract you from this, especially when you have progressed to the writing stage. You will undoubtedly have other commitments and obligations in your life. You may be working a demanding job. You may have a teaching or research assistantship that puts demands on your time. You may have a family life that requires your attention to small children, teenagers, aging parents, or a needy spouse (or all of the above!). One of the strategies that will get you to your end goal is to put all aspects and interests in your life into a healthy perspective. We suggest that you carve out time for those things and people who are most important to you so you maintain a healthy balance in your life while meeting the demands of a doctoral student.

Maximize writing efficiency. Many students take longer than necessary to complete their dissertations simply due to procrastination. The research and writing process can be hard and even discouraging. Getting started with an idea for a research topic is where many students flounder. Because the process of starting a writing assignment requires a large amount of energy and concentration, students tend to wait for a large chunk of uninterrupted time to begin the assignment. Then they discover that days have passed without anything being written. Another area where students waste time is with construction of the literature review. Some of the reason for this black hole of time is that students begin the process without receiving adequate guidance about how to most effectively approach a literature review. Therefore, many students will pick up and read at length any written work that has anything to do with the research topic. Your discussion of the literature in your field does not equate to summarizing everything that has been written on the subject. There are smart ways to approach writing a literature review. Your major professor and other faculty in your department can help guide you.

Why is it important to build a solid support structure?

Like many education majors, Doug was not looking forward to working through the statistical aspects of his dissertation. He was required to take two statistics classes as part of the core curriculum for the program, and the faculty were absolutely wonderful at teaching statistics in a way that made sense. At the time Doug was ready to conduct a statistical analysis of his research data, there were many cobwebs in his brain from the statistics classes he had completed a year prior. He needed help. Fortunately, his college offered a service where graduate students in the Department of Research and Measurement would hold office hours to assist students with questions about research methods and statistical analysis as a supplement to the guidance from a major professor. He scheduled two appointments but came away from those sessions still somewhat lost.

The importance of a mentoring network. An important key to succeeding in many aspects of your graduate program is developing and nurturing relationships with other graduate students, with faculty, and with administrators and staff at your institution. While your major professor may provide the oversight and guidance for your research, there may be other individuals (faculty or not) who can better assist you in other areas (career, writing, speaking, networking, research methods, etc.). Identifying and getting to know those individuals early into your program will facilitate your ability to discover important and very helpful information not only about your specific program but also about potential employment opportunities, financial assistance resources, and research opportunities. Good relationships with faculty at your home institution may lead them to introduce you or recommend you to their colleagues in other departments and at other universities.

Doug is a great case study in this regard. Although he took an active approach to solve his statistics issue, it still did not provide the needed clarity. So he turned to his mentoring network, and one of his mentors introduced him to Dr. Banion, a faculty member from a completely different college. Dr. Banion asked Doug about the area of his research and, upon learning of Doug's struggle with statistics, offered his assistance. Working with Dr.

Banion, Doug was able to accomplish in one hour what he wasn't able to accomplish going through old notes from his statistics class or working with the help center. Also, collaborating with a knowledgeable faculty member helped Doug gain greater confidence in his networking ability.

Regardless of the career path you want to take, building a network of scholars and professionals will be greatly beneficial to your development. If you are a natural introvert, it may require conscious effort to take the initiative to get to know the students and faculty in your program. There may even be workshops you can take that help you to develop this key skill. So even though it may be tempting to form a small clique with other students, it is to your benefit to cast a wide net when it comes to working on projects. You never know when you will develop a relationship with someone who becomes a prolific partner with you in research, writing, or career development. One of the greatest opportunities you have as a doctoral student is the ability to develop relationships with individuals who can help you overcome areas where you may be struggling.

Engage with other graduate students. Make the effort to get to know and befriend other graduate students early on. Especially seek out those who have similar needs and are in similar situations as you, whether you are married, international, or from a population that may be underrepresented in the discipline. These students may be knowledgeable about other students who have graduated and what they are doing now. They can tell you which professors have been most successful obtaining funding for research and mentoring students. Fellow graduate students, particularly those who have been around longer than you, are a valuable source of information about issues such as department politics and faculty personalities and their teaching and mentoring styles. Also, if you are brand new to the university, fellow graduate students can lead you to viable housing options, the best places to eat on a budget, and childcare facilities if you are moving and raising a family. It can also be helpful to build networks with graduate students outside your immediate department. Many universities have graduate student associations that offer occasional social and professional development events that provide a great networking opportunity. It is through these interactions that you will begin to understand any struggles you may be having are not unique!

Your socialization into the academic community of your home department is also an important component to successfully completing the degree. It is through the socialization process that students ask themselves whether the benefit is greater than the cost and struggles associated with the degree journey. Students who identify themselves as members of the academic community within their discipline will feel a sense of belonging. Students who do not feel like part of the community associated with their particular discipline will have difficulty persevering through the more trying times. It is OK, and even normal when you feel particularly stressed, to question whether you made the right decision in pursuing the long journey to a doctoral degree. However, when questions of uncertainty and doubt begin to consume your thoughts, take action. Talk to those closest to you, and revisit some of the action exercises provided in the book. It is also important to note that most universities have student counseling centers to support all levels of students with a variety of needs and concerns.

How do I overcome feelings of self-doubt and frustration?

My-Lien was struggling with her motivation to remain in the biomedical engineering doctoral program. She was doing outstanding work in her courses and had already been a coauthor on a peer-reviewed publication. I knew her major professor, and he indicated that she was not fully engaged with the other students in the lab and had confided to him that she was homesick and did not have any local family support since she was an international student. I was able to convince My-Lien to make an appointment at the counseling center, and I also reached out to one of the staff in the international student office. They were able to get her involved in an international student support group, and she ultimately remained in the program and earned her degree.

Completing a doctoral degree is arguably one of the most challenging, difficult, frustrating, exhilarating, yet fulfilling journeys you will ever take. Throughout the other chapters, we have provided insights into the rigors of the journey and offered suggestions that will help smooth the way. Still, it is expected for you to feel stressed and frustrated from time to time along the way. For many, the challenges seem so overwhelming that giving up the pursuit appears to be the best option. But as with My-Lien, there are always university support programs and caring faculty, staff, and administrators who are there to help.

There are steps you can take to minimize some of the common psycho-logical challenges students encounter. Some graduate students have difficulty adjusting to the prospect that their research and methodology will be under constant judgment and criticism from faculty and peers. Welcome to aca-demia. By its very nature, research must be presented so others can question it. Although there are some faculty who take delight in challenging anyone about anything in a sometimes negative way, the process of critical review is essential to good research and to the development of the researcher. While the criticism may *seem* personal because it is *your* research, the critical review is about the product and process, not the person. If you want to develop into an exceptional researcher, a thick skin is required, as is the idea that perfection is unattainable. There is no such thing as a perfect dissertation or research proj-ect. Strive for perfection and the highest quality of work with every project, but subscribe to the idea that someone will always find flaws in your product. In addition, you can operate only within the limits of the money, energy, time, and support realistically available to you.

If you feel your motivation and energy wane, remind yourself of the larger picture and why you entered the journey of a doctoral degree. Revisit your vi-sion statement, and instead of thinking about the deadlines and requirements, think about the contributions you are making as a scholar. Focus on the val-ues of the journey, such as the exciting nature of the complex issues you are studying, the valuable skills you are developing as a critical thinker and writer, the ability to develop those skills in someone else, the conflict of ideas with which you are engaging that lead to stimulating debate and developments of new knowledge, and working collaboratively with others who are curious about issues in your field. It is important to recognize that moments of doubt and low confidence are natural. Do not, however, wallow in this place for too long. Instead, use those moments for a brief time of reflection and creative space; then move back into a productive zone. This is where your network of mentors and supporters can encourage you out of any ruts and help validate your reasons for the journey. Most importantly, don't let the feelings of doubt overwhelm you or convince you that you should not be pursuing a degree.

What time-management strategies will help me to finish more quickly?

Ever the perfectionist, Ren had completed his graduate program in history with a 4.00 average in all his required courses. His research was good, and he had presented it at several national meetings, but he had only one low-impact peer-reviewed publication. In contrast, his fiancée, Joan, had also graduated from the program, and although her GPA was 3.14, she had several publications that had received some national attention and a well-developed plan for what the next phase of the project would be. When Joan began to get interviews for faculty positions, Ren could not understand why he was not as competitive when his graduate transcript was superior to hers.

Course grades, priorities, and what truly matters. Most graduate programs require core coursework and a 3.00 average GPA to remain in good academic standing. However, when you graduate with your doctoral degree, your degree will be worth no less if you finished your coursework with a 3.00 GPA or a 4.00 GPA. The university transcript simply validates your degree, and not a soul will ever ask you about the grade you received in Stats I five years ago. You are, of course, responsible to obtain a solid foundation of knowledge in your area of study and to demonstrate an ability to articulate your level of knowledge to a satisfactory level with at least a 3.00 GPA. But there is a difference between working toward increasing your knowledge and getting buried in the minutia of completing every detail of every assignment to absolute perfection. If you are already in a doctoral program, you may have discovered that the rules of the game as a graduate student are different from what you experienced in your undergraduate career. The true priority is on your research and writing. As Ren discovered, no one was evaluating him for a job based on his course grades; he was being evaluated on what he had done as a researcher, the quality of his productivity, and how he could advance the field. The same is true if you do not intend to get a job in academia. You will be expected to demonstrate that you can "work the problem," take a project from development to completion, have great communication skills, and lead. Your ability as a researcher is what gets you to the table, not an A in the research design course.

Our point here is not that it's OK to slough off your courses. You succeeded in your undergraduate program as well as your master's degree partially because you are the type of person who attends to detail and is not happy with turning in work that is not your very best effort. The takeaway message is about prioritizing your energies to the assignments and projects that will have the biggest impact. For example, you will be asked by the faculty to read copious materials. It is simply not possible to read every word of every book and relevant article in the discipline. You will need to develop strategies that will help you skim through book chapters and articles to obtain a sufficient understanding of the content. Always strive for excellence, but it may be that the time you put into your research project, as opposed to earning an A in a course, will be a much better use of your time.

Find a productive study space that belongs to you. While it is nice to study within the comforts of your home, it can also be a place of distraction and slow down your progress. The reality is that regardless of your role within your household or place of residence, there are household jobs that belong to you. This may include laundry, car maintenance, cleaning, cooking, or a number of other duties. Even if you possess a huge amount of self-discipline, when you are in your routine environment, your mind and body will expect you to engage in activities associated with that environment. If you are at a difficult place in your studies, such as a writing assignment you are dreading, you will become even more easily distracted. You cannot allow this to happen to you, but there are several approaches you can take that will dramatically improve your efficiency and productivity.

First, it is essential that you have a place you can go that is exclusively your study or workspace. When you are within its environment, your mind and body will know you are there to work. If you have not used this approach before, it may take some time to train your mind, but it will ultimately work for you. The space could be a set location within the library, an assigned desk within your department, or a secluded area in a university building. If you must work at home, get a desk, and carve out a defined space where the only thing you do when you sit there is study, analyze your research, and write. If you spend any time on your computer surfing the web and engaging in social media, this can become a distraction. Depending on your level of self-discipline, you may want to buy a computer to use in your workspace that becomes solely a tool for writing, nothing else. Alternatively, many libraries have laptops students can borrow for free. In the context of these suggestions, it is critical to understand that the writing of the dissertation will take several months. If you can't carve out long periods of focused time where you are fully dedicated to the writing, the timeline to completion will increase exponentially.

Reward yourself. Another important strategy is to establish a rewards program with yourself. The way this works is that you reward yourself with something you enjoy for the completion of an assignment or benchmark. Using the social media example from the previous section, it may be that you reward yourself thirty minutes of time on Facebook for every six hours of writing you complete. We used strategies like this quite often when completing our dissertations and used movies as a reward for completing major milestones. This approach can help create some additional motivation and reduce procrastination.

Find the best time when you are the most focused. Finally, identify times of the day and days of the week when you are the most productive and can set aside at least two hours at a time to devote to specific areas of your project. For periods of one hour or less, we recommend you spend that time on items that will not require complex thinking or creativity. It can take several minutes to really get into your groove with a train of thought. If you can, reserve your most brain-intensive work for sessions where you can devote two hours or more. Be sure to take intermittent breaks during long study sessions. Breaks do not need to be rigidly scheduled and should not interrupt creative or productive work. When you come to a natural break, take advantage of it by getting up and walking around, in some fresh air if possible. We found that the "breaks" where we tried to clear our minds were the times we would actually get some of our best ideas.

Carlos was required to take two semesters of statistics courses. His advisor recommended he take the courses early in the program sequence because it would help him to better understand, evaluate, and critique research articles. However, some of the other graduate students advised that he wait to take statistics until he had a solid research topic established for his project. They reasoned that he would better grasp the statistical methods if he could apply his learning to actual research questions. Also, they argued that the material would be fresh in his mind when he was ready to apply it to his own research and take the qualifying exams.

Timing your required course sequence. Developing a clear strategy for your required courses can enhance your ability to get through the program in the least possible amount of time. Carlos's advisor recommended he take statistics right away, and this is good advice because, regardless of your discipline, understanding methods and analysis is critical to developing your skills as a scholar and researcher. However, if your research project depends on the application of methods you will derive from a specific course, there is also a benefit to waiting to take it until you have a good handle on your research plan. The benefit is in the way you learn the material. Some students learn best when they can immediately apply the lesson to a practical problem, but the way courses are offered and scheduled may always be favorable. Thus, the earlier you have a defined research plan, the better you will be able to see the connection to the course material and apply these perspectives to your research.

Capturing your ideas. Be prepared to capture extraneous thoughts when they occur. All the different mobile devices available today allow for immediate recording of any thought that might pop into your head. For example, some people find that exercise helps them generate creative juices. If this is you and you tend to exercise away from home, make sure you have a way to record your thoughts as soon as they come to you.

What skills and tools will help me to finish?

Ellen had always been above average when it came to retaining informa-tion and taking tests. Her presentation and public-speaking skills were also strong. But as she started her doctoral program in anthropology, the writing requirements made her nervous. Writing had never been Ellen's strength, and she always had issues with actually starting any writing assignment. Solving this problem by improving her general writing skills was something she knew she would need to do to complete the program.

Most of us are just like Ellen. We all have some aspect of writing that we don't enjoy or haven't fully developed. The majority of students and faculty we have talked to and trained, regardless of the level of success they have had in aca-demia or the private sector, list writing as one of their least favorite activities. However, being a good writer is probably the one skill that is most directly correlated to success in graduate school and beyond. A dissertation, grant proposal, patent application, book manuscript, white paper, summary report, journal article, screenplay, or even an e-mail message represents an outcome of productivity, and the quality will be used to judge you throughout your entire career. Regardless of your discipline, coherent writing is an essential skill you must embrace and continually work at. In graduate school, writing about what you think and what the research has to say about a topic is a major component of the journey.

Learning to love writing. Writing is not easy and can almost always be improved. The more you engage in the process and practice the activity, the better you will get and the more conformable you will feel. Therefore, en-gaging in writing exercises outside of the requirements placed on you by the major professor or your courses is advantageous. For example, you may find it helpful to keep a learning journal. A learning journal can help you form and record the learning and insights you are developing. Alternatively, just keep a journal, and write about whatever is motivating or interesting to you in the moment. You will find that the process of just taking time to write can help bring clarity to thoughts you are having but cannot seem to bring together in any coherent fashion. As you go through the process of honing in on your research topic, writing your thoughts on a daily basis can be especially helpful and can actually help you begin sections of your research proposal. We recommend you keep a notepad or mobile device with you to capture notes and ideas so you can later reflect on them or share them with your major professor and dissertation committee.

> *We were about thirty minutes into the reflective writing exercise for incoming freshman in the STEM Academy program. Looking around the room, it appeared to be a death march, and I heard comments such as "I'm a science major. Why are we doing this exercise?" The workshop facilitator was doing her best to provide context to the exercise, but it was clear that most of the students were not buying into its application and did not feel it was relevant to their trajectory as STEM majors. After the session was over, however, several students approached us to say they fully enjoyed the activity but did not want to speak up since they were embarrassed to admit this in front of other science peers. Later in the semester, numerous students came through the office and commented on how the writing exercise had helped them in their coursework.*

It's not always easy to see the application for what you are doing in the moment. But *any* writing exercises and a disciplined approach to the process will have inherent value. We have found that students have different preferences when it comes to writing. Some will write down ideas and create rough drafts as they read supporting material. Others prefer to read everything that is relevant to the topic before they write a word. Whatever approach you take, you should discipline yourself to set a cutoff for your reading and carve out time to write down your impressions. There are so many great books and articles that have been published on any given topic, and it is great to be well-read, but as was stated previously, it simply is not possible to read everything. If you are not satisfied with beginning any writing exercise until you have completely exhausted all the materials available on the topic, it will be very difficult to make any progress in developing the writing skills required to complete the assignment and the degree program. Ellen recognized early that she was not the best writer, but she was able to take advantage of the university writing center and several professional development workshops offered by the graduate school. Ellen also developed a relationship with a graduate student in the PhD program in English who was willing to mentor her and help her learn various exercises to overcome her challenges.

Think of the projects you have been involved with that have had the best outcomes and individuals you have worked with who have been able to get the best out of you. What was consistent about these experiences? When we do this exercise with students, a recurring theme is that the most successful projects always start with a great plan. In addition, the manager of the project sets realistic benchmarks of productivity and keeps everyone accountable for achieving the outcomes. Now think about your graduate program and the trajectory of its completion. In many ways, you are serving the role of both the project manager and the workforce to get it done. The best strategy for staying on task is to develop a plan, set benchmarks, and stay organized.

A great way to start a major writing project (i.e., dissertation or research paper) is to work backward from the due date or the date you expect to earn the degree and set defined long-range, midrange, and short-range benchmarks. If this type of activity is not part of your skill set yet, think of the most self-disciplined and organized person you know. Seek them out, and have them show you how to develop a goal-oriented plan. This may be someone from your mentoring team, a fellow student, or an advisor. Once a plan is developed, you will also need to set up an accountability system that requires you to report your progress. If you are not in a situation where you are required to provide updates on a weekly basis, you should identify someone who will hold you accountable to make progress and ensure you are spending your time wisely. This should be someone close to you who will ask you what you have accomplished on your research project on at least a weekly basis.

Chapter 5 action items

One of the obvious skills that will help you complete your degree more quickly is effective time management. There are entire books written on this subject, and if you feel that your skills are not where they need to be, you may want to invest in some additional training in this area. However, for the purpose of this book, we will highlight and summarize what we believe to be some of the most important behaviors to keep you on track.

ACADEMIC PLANNING EXERCISE AND ACTION PLAN.

1. <u>Use every class and every assignment to build on the literature review.</u> The literature review is the foundation of a dissertation. The process of constructing it will help you in a number of ways:
   - It helps you identify the topics of greatest interest to you.
   - You will become familiar with how established scholars use literature reviews in presenting their research.
   - Each article you read will provide you with ideas for your dissertation topic as you identify gaps in the research.
   - Each work's bibliography will guide you to other publications related to your topic of interest.
   - You will identify leading scholars in the field.

2. <u>Let technology be your ally.</u> It is important to have a high-quality and reliable computer that can do everything you need to be productive, so invest in a quality computer and a hard drive with sufficient memory so you can store and organize your electronic references. Additionally, one of the biggest time wasters is trying to find bibliographical information for citations. There are great electronic resources available these days that can greatly help to streamline this process; however, it is up to you to make sure the sources you consult are incorporated

into the program you choose. Your university librarians are ready and willing to help you learn how to use this program, so make time to meet with one of them. Trust me: the small amount of time you invest in learning how to work with programs like RefWorks will pay off in dividends. Also, save, save, save your work. Get in the habit, if you are not already, of saving every few minutes. It doesn't take any time to do, and you will be thankful at some point that you did. With the capabilities of technology, there is no reason why any of your work should ever be lost. One strategy is to e-mail the latest draft of any assignment to yourself at least daily. That way, if the document is destroyed on your hard drive or flash drive, you will always be able to access the latest draft by merely logging on to your e-mail. There is no worse feeling than to have spent precious time on something that is lost forever. Don't let that happen to you. It is a huge waste of time and effort and is 100 percent preventable.

3. <u>Develop lean time-management skills</u>. Don't perform an action or task more than once. For instance, too much time is wasted on reading the same articles over again or digging for a reference. Develop a method to keep track of your references as you read and take notes. An online resource such as RefWorks is a wonderful tool, and the investment of time up front to become comfortable with it will save you a lot of time and frustration on the back end.

4. <u>Have a good plan</u>. It is not uncommon for the unexpected to happen during the course of your doctoral journey. The research question that you have had your heart on exploring turns out to be completely unfeasible for your dissertation, or your major advisor, who was the reason for your studying at a particular university, is leaving the institution. These "surprises" can range from fairly minor situations to major catastrophes. However, if you have a good plan that includes alternative strategies if something goes awry, you will minimize the time that is consumed in getting back on track.

5. <u>Organize your references</u>. When you come across publications that are closely associated with your topic, always review the references

listed at the end. Other people's references are sometimes overlooked but are a logical way for you to find additional sources of information. This review will help you get a good idea of which publications are being cited regularly and what is considered important in the field. Another important strategy for saving time is to start organizing your references from the very beginning. Most university libraries offer a free database program that you can use to organize all the references you review for your dissertation. They will typically provide free training classes on how to use these databases. Take advantage of that; it is a good investment of your time.

Afterword

While a book on the topic of graduate degree completion cannot possibly address every situation you may encounter, we believe this book covers the most common barriers to completion and strategies to facilitate a successful process toward the finish line. Earning a graduate degree can be one of the most rewarding experiences in a person's life, and both of us have taken significantly different paths to our PhD degrees and careers. Our paths were not easy, and it is important to note that the stories we have shared are all from real-life situations we have personally experienced or helped others overcome. We hope you found these stories and the action exercises included at the end of each chapter helpful. We both feel that our paths could have been smoother had we known the information we have put into this book. There will always be barriers, but we have always found that we learn a great deal from what others have done and that focused planning based on authentic information is a conduit for success—and if you know challenges are coming, it is way easier to avoid or minimize them.

We feel the information in this book will be useful for all stages of graduate school, from preadmission to graduation. Keep it in a place where you can easily access it, and refer to the sections that are most pertinent to your current situation. This is your journey; make the most of it. Also, be forward thinking. The past is past and cannot be changed. Although difficulties and frustrations may be close at hand, if you look past them and see the rewards for completing the degree, then the obstacles become worth overcoming. A couple of years' worth of effort to finish the dissertation can provide a wealth of career opportunities from which you may reap a lifetime's worth of rewards.

Best wishes for a successful graduate school experience!

About the Authors

*H*olly J. Schoenherr, PhD, is the director of human resources for Pinellas County, Florida. She has sixteen years of experience in higher education, serving in both academic and administrative positions at the University of South Florida, Rice University, and St. Cloud State University. Schoenherr received her doctorate in higher education administration from the University of South Florida. She completed her master's and doctoral degrees while working full time and raising two children.

Richard S. Pollenz, PhD, is a professor at the University of South Florida. He has spent much of his twenty-five-year career finding innovative ways to inspire students to what is possible. He has managed both graduate education and undergraduate research programs. Pollenz received his doctorate from Northwestern University. He is a fellow of the American Association for the Advancement of Science and has been recognized for his research in molecular toxicology.

Resources

Web resources

American Association of Medical Colleges (AAMC)
aamc.org

Reports and statistics on medical school admissions. Essential information for anyone interested in attending medical school.

Chronicle of Higher Education
http://www.chronicle.com/

One of the major national publications regarding higher education. Searchable archives for reports and commentary regarding trends and outcomes across higher education.

Council of Graduate Schools (CGS)
cgsnet.org

Reports on all aspects of graduate education.

Georgetown University: Center on Education and the Workforce
cew.georgetown.edu

The Georgetown University Center on Education and the Workforce is an independent, nonprofit research and policy institute affiliated with the Georgetown McCourt School of Public Policy that studies the link between education, career qualifications, and workforce demands. There are several excellent reports that can help inform career choices.

National Center for Education Statistics (NCES)
nces.ed.gov

The National Center for Education Statistics (NCES) is the primary federal entity for collecting and analyzing data related to education. If you want the data on education trends and outcomes, this is the site to explore.

Peterson's Guide to Graduate Schools
petersons.com/graduate-schools

A resource to quickly identify graduate programs and university information at the start of your search process.

US Department of Labor
dol.gov

Official government site of labor statistics and projections. A wealth of interesting and useful information.

Books we have found to be helpful in graduate school decision making and that are excellent supplements to this book.

Career guidance in STEM

Put Your Science to Work: The Take-Charge Career Guide for Scientists—Practical Advice. Peter S. Fiske, PhD. 2000. ISBN: 978-0875902951.

Uncovering Truffles: The Scarcity and Value of Women in STEM. Melanie Polkosky, PhD. 2015. ISBN 978-1515304289.

What Color Is Your Parachute? Richard N. Bolles. 2016. ISBN 978-1607746621.

Completing the dissertation

The Dissertation Journey: A Practical and Comprehensive Guide to Planning, Writing, and Defending Your Dissertation. Carol M. Roberts. 2010. ISBN 978-1412977982.

Made in the USA
San Bernardino, CA
26 June 2017